ALCOHOL RECOVERY

Make You a Simple and Effective Alcohol Addiction

(Control Alcohol and Love Life More: Discover Freedom & Change Your Life)

Richard Phan

Published By Richard Phan

Richard Phan

All Rights Reserved

Alcohol Recovery: Make You a Simple and Effective Alcohol Addiction (Control Alcohol and Love Life More: Discover Freedom & Change Your Life)

ISBN 978-1-77485-379-5

All rights reserved. No part of this guide may be reproduced in any form without permission in writing from the publisher except in the case of brief quotations embodied in critical articles or reviews.

Legal & Disclaimer

The information contained in this book is not designed to replace or take the place of any form of medicine or professional medical advice. The information in this book has been provided for educational and entertainment purposes only.

The information contained in this book has been compiled from sources deemed reliable, and it is accurate to the best of the Author's knowledge; however, the Author cannot guarantee its accuracy and validity and cannot be held liable for any errors or omissions. Changes are periodically made to this book. You must consult your doctor or get professional medical advice before using any of the suggested remedies, techniques, or information in this book.

Upon using the information contained in this book, you agree to hold harmless the Author from and against any damages, costs, and expenses, including any legal fees potentially resulting from the application of any of the information provided by this guide. This disclaimer applies to any damages or injury caused by the use and application, whether directly or indirectly, of any advice or information presented, whether for breach of contract, tort, negligence, personal injury, criminal intent, or under any other cause of action.

You agree to accept all risks of using the information presented inside this book. You need to consult a professional medical practitioner in order to ensure you are both able and healthy enough to participate in this program.

TABLE OF CONTENTS

INTRODUCTION 1

CHAPTER 1: STOP DRINKING 3

CHAPTER 2: ILLNESS OR WEAKNESS? 7

CHAPTER 3: ALTER YOUR WAY OF THINKING 21

CHAPTER 4: WHAT IS THE REASON WE DRINK 27

CHAPTER 5: DANGERS TO BEWARE OF 34

CHAPTER 6: THE EFFECTS OF ALCOHOLISM EXPLAINED ... 54

CHAPTER 7: SIGNS OF ALCOHOLISM 62

CHAPTER 8: HEALTH DAMAGES DUE TO ALCOHOL CONSUMPTION 71

CHAPTER 9: TELL YOUR FAMILY AND FRIENDS 81

CHAPTER 10: BENEFITS OF QUITTING 92

CHAPTER 11: DRINK OR DON'T DRINK 110

CHAPTER 12: DEALING WITH THE EFFECTS OF ALCOHOL WITHDRAWAL 128

CHAPTER 13: THE TREATMENTS FOR ALCOHOL USE DISORDER 132

CHAPTER 14: MEDICATIONS FOR ALCOHOLISM TREATMENT 139

CHAPTER 15: THE SUPER SELF-CONFIDENCE SPELL 148

CHAPTER 16: FINDING NEW HABITS 165

CHAPTER 17: HELPING AND HELP AND 169

CHAPTER 18: SIMPLE TIPS TO QUIT DRINKING 172

CONCLUSION 184

Introduction

If you're ready to quit drinking, but you aren't able to do this, you're not alone.It's very difficult to put the end of your enjoyment with alcohol-based beverages.But there are a lot of ways to begin living the way you want to live in a healthy manner that allows you to feel great consistently again!

Drinking a drink after a long day's work is a great method of unwinding. However, you've probably figured out the way that one drink could be followed by a number of others and this is the time when alcohol really starts to hinder you from your potential.

You will be taught all about the effects of alcohol on to your body, brain, emotions and money.Then I will guide you through certain strategies that will assist you in slowing down your drinking or even stop completely.You will also discover amazing ways to keep your body strong as well as your mind stronger as you move along your journey.So continue reading as this book is perfect for those who want to be more informed and healthier in dealing with alcohol.

Chapter 1: Stop drinking

The addiction to alcohol is not new. Due to various circumstances in their lives, people are dependent on alcohol, and this dependence has changed their lives. Many depend on drinking to get over their issues and other drinkers drink to boost their confidence. Others claim that they drink occasionally , yet they seek out occasions to use as excuses to drink. Whatever the motives for making an individual addicted to alcohol, the dependence must be stopped. It's not simple to get over addiction, especially with alcohol, especially when drinking is your sole reason for living.

If you are:

If you've been in an accident, or have been detained for drinking and driving

Problems in your relationships because of drinking alcohol

Have issues in your school, job or your career because of drinking alcohol

Have financial issues because of drinking alcohol

I've had health problems due to drinking alcohol

Have you ever felt stressed and depressed due to drinking alcohol

Do you want to start an entirely new life, without the use of alcohol

This guide is just for you!

Like in any addiction treatment program, acknowledging that you have an addiction problem and require help is the initial step in recovery. Denial won't bring you anywhere. It is imperative to be brave enough to defend yourself to fight the addiction. Yes, you can!

WARNING:

It's not an easy task to stop drinking. The majority of people who would like to quit, stopped trying after about a week. But, if you stop today, what are you going to accomplish? You'll find yourself going through the same problems again and you'll feel depressed and depressed.

For people who are heavy drinkers There is a particular time frame known as the withdrawal phase in an alcohol rehabilitation program. In the withdrawal phase, you experience uncomfortable symptoms because alcohol is leaving your body completely. It is another cause many people who wish to stop drinking drink alcohol once more.

This phase is merely an element of your recovery. Everybody gets through it and there is a good chance that once alcohol has gone from your system, you'll be feeling much better. The withdrawal phase can take a few days or weeks, depending on the severity of the addict's dependence on alcohol.

You need a strong help system throughout your recovery from drinking. It is possible to manage this on your own however having someone who you can trust in your corner makes all the impact!

It is important to seek out professional assistance for medical problems or think you require a professional guide to help you overcome the addiction to alcohol.

Positive thinking is essential! Positive thinking can help you stay focused and reach your goals.

Chapter 2: Illness Or Weakness?

If a person does not admit being sick, but it is apparent that it can only be acknowledged by you, then this person will be able to let go of the feeling of shame over the incident. Alcoholism is a disease characterized by altered morality. Following a drinking spree the person feels embarrassed of what transpired. People are shocked by the fact that it was not embarrassing to drink? When you're under the influence of the urge to drink, it was embarrassing, however "craving" (the scientific term for compulsive drive) is thought of by the sick to be one of its basic demands. The old mechanism is brought into effect: "ashamed, but what do I take?" After getting intoxicated the shame is gone completely. Man is already becoming a creature. After an indulgence and feeling of shame, it is not just one.

When they feel ashamed of a issue Patients are unable to not just solve the issue but also to even begin to address the issue. It's difficult to deal with the things you're embarrassed of. Alcoholics are similar to a person who sweeps the cockroaches off a sofa only to never see them. He'll be required to discuss this topic of conversation for the rest of his life with either silly laughter (often you'll witness adults giggling as if they were schoolchildren whenever this subject is brought up) or even theorizing (resonant thinking on the philosophy, biochemistry and the historical roots of the phenomenon) or in plain denial. It's a matter of choice After about two or three sentences it will be some sort of "Well that's enough with this!"

People who are concerned about the treatment of patients don't want to discuss the issue. They think that, once more it's not worthwhile to provoke. The man has already appeared like a pity. And if they are not happy about the situation, but it's best to forget and carry in the present.

For one thing, forgetting won't be a success, not just because it's impossible to remember and also because it occurs again. We will deal with the consequences, but without changing the cause.

If an alcohol user is ill and pleads The feeling of shame is a thing of the past. There's no reason to be ashamed of the illness. In the end, nobody is embarrassed by bronchial asthma or hypertension. It's true that you shouldn't talk to everyone about this subject. Some will be offended However, it's not the case for everyone.

There are close relatives, people who know everything and if they don't understand anything "tell your story" is a standard phrase used by close family members.

There are people who have had to deal with this issue. They'll be able to react in a manner that's right and will not laugh or act rude. Talking to such a person can be extremely beneficial. A lot of them would like to share their experience and are grateful for those who listen to them.

Finally, there doctors who comprehend the patient and show empathy for them is their duty as a professional. It's foolish to feel ashamed of a doctor. In any event, if you don't get over the shame of your feelings then you are not going to achieve anything at all. It is impossible to lift yourself off of the ground where you're standing with your back to.

If he admits that he's sick, one is able to let go of guilt. In reality, refusing means to be lost. The feelings won't disappear instantly and certainly they will not last forever. Importantly, the patient stops taking these feelings into consideration in his reasoning. He recognizes that they are feelings of pain. This is what his illness is hidden from him. Alcoholism is indeed a mental illness that is psychiatric, or it is a form of madness. But the drunk isn't in any way guilty.

A person who is a alcoholic feels forever guilt-ridden. Sometimes, he believes that it's a good thing to help him quit drinking. Some, in general tend to cultivate this belief with positive intentions, hoping that this will help bring the person closer to sobriety and treatment. It is commonplace to inform the patient's shortcomings, to scold him or point out his flaws, and in a nutshell to make him feel like an infant. It's actually contrary!

In the beginning, when a person thinks that he is not sick and guilty (and they are not the same thing) and then he'll find excuses. A person who is a drinker becomes an unlucky individual who protects the person who kills him, alcohol. He has to explain to everyone and himself the reason he was drinking? Alcoholic alibis start to be constructed, each one more absurd than the next (such an existence or job and a wife like that and so on.). The public begins to debate about this issue: "it's not so bad that you can't drink like I do." The arguments are endless and ineffective. There are no excuses , because there aren't any accusations. You may think you are sick, and yes, it is insane, but if this is a disease, and it is the disease that is the cause. Nobody is justified in the case that he suffers from toothache or was a radiculitis-related attack. If you choose to keep the belief that it's not a condition and it's a sign that you live your life as. It's true that we don't want it however, what you are able to choose to do is up to you...

It is not necessary to think about what the motives of a thief who took everything. Sure, he's the burglar! But, the question is: what made it so easy to penetrate? There was no security.

Furthermore, if one believes that he is guilty, they'll think that they have not been offered assistance, but rather punishment. If you're guilty you are penalized! At present the alcoholic is adamant against all manipulatives and influences. He can't afford to seek help since the person believes that he is "not sufficiently guilty." The entire discussion on this subject is irritating. The way people view the subject has changed The advice received is seen as jokes, reproaches or as a joke even the word "alcoholic," invariably, as a derogatory term.

"Why you bother me?" is a very frequent question at this point. The ideal answer is: "why does a person visit dental clinic?" It may even hurt however, they don't bring the patient in with pressure, the patients themselves make. The logic of this is maintained until guilt gets so severe that it becomes more likely to be punished. The punishment itself is attractive as it eases the moment of guilt. It's not like they're punished twice. I had another drink - and the discussion was shut in a hospital for the second time.

"The "poor fellow" performed the procedure, but then, the wreckage starts The situation is so complicated that we can't obtain what we did not think we would get. When I was a patient in the hospital and received my punishment. The patient will suffer throughout the year, suffering in pain, and afflict himself and other people, and he's worse off because that's what he got! At times, at the close of the year the family starts with a whisper "He must drink after the treatment is over. Another drink! He was able to pull his emotional spring on a full year. Now he has let go. ..." The events that occurred are associated with alcohol mythology. everybody has heard of the person or family member who's story ended similar to the way. The outcome of such a situation is not considered to be positive, it's only a shift on the amount of disturbances however, it is it is not always. However, this does not mean you are not required to seek out help. It is essential to recognize that the outcome is 90% contingent on the technique however on what the patient was educated about. If the patient is at fault and is punished, the result will be punishment. If he's sick, it's about help, delivery and then he will improve.

Thirdly, if the alcoholic believes that he is not guilty, but not sick and guilty, he is bound to rectify his mistakes until he drink. This is the fate of alcoholics , people who are adamant about drinking. They do not just consume a lot of alcohol, but they also read, work, have a frenzied love affair like it's an additional binge. When they emerge from an alcohol nightmare, feeling a huge feeling of guilt, one begins to look for an accomplishment. He is in need of extreme fatigue, as only extreme fatigue can aid in removing guilt. What are the most frequent comments you hear about patients' experiences: "Well, what an drunk I am, I'm working!"

Naturally, it is how you do work in the way you work! You have to feed yourself, not just you but also your alcohol addiction. The problem is that thoughts are. In the end, we're discussing a condition, and it's likely to progress. With increasing speed, at some point, patients reach the point of exhaustion and a new breakdown occurs. This is a vicious loop or more accurately, it's a spiral that leads down. In the arena, people move in the manner of circus horse riders for many years and years. Alcoholism can be a very clever host. He doesn't care about the swift loss of life for his slaves. So, they live fairly long. If nothing happens to them trauma, poisoning and other reasons for early death - an alcohol user can live between 60 or 70 years. However, during throughout his life the person does not live and feeds the illness. He is a student, a married person and has children, but throughout his life, he's in two states, or, if he is not aware, preparing for an addiction, or engaged in the middle of one. There's just one method to escape from this roller coaster of madness : to acknowledge that you're sick. In this situation sobriety isn't an opportunity to make amends instead, it is a chance to start living life as was intended. Every person was created to be happy, but those who drink cannot afford it.

When drinking alcohol, one is destined to live a life that is in a state of discontent or drunk. Sober, an alcoholic should be happy. In the event that he is not, he'll be drunk. This isn't just a desire or a suggestion from a doctor with the possibility of saving lives!

When he admits that he's sick, an individual is able to let go of guilt and shame. They can be replaced with respectability.

Sobriety is a virtue that is best for people who can appreciate. There's a variance in this belief. Don't be offended by someone who, upon hearing an admission that "I haven't had a drink in the last six months,"" responds: "so what?" If you are talking to someone who hasn't been drinking in five years they is likely to reply with: "I remember the first six months ... Bravo Keep it up! going!

This is true pride. Not extravagant, but a special. Please forgive those who don't comprehend this. Most of them aren't drinking addicts, they don't know, and are not required to comprehend this. The majority of those who don't understand are people suffering from illness who haven't admitted to themselves. We'll be pitying them, God wills and one day they will get this joy.

The most significant conclusion you can draw when you realize that you are an addict is the desire to end drinking alcohol permanently. This means, for the rest of your the rest of your life, you should not drink any alcohol of any amount in any form, for any reason. In this instance we're talking about complete sobriety.

In the field of narcology, there are two main pillars that are essential to narcology that are active involvement of the patient, and total sobriety that results from it. If someone provides "dose control"," "treatment with no expertise," or any other "help" the person is not considered"a doctor," regardless of how they introduce himself.

The requirement of absolute sobriety was not the advice of a physician it is a condition of a person who is sick! It is doubtful that anyone has heard the patient convinced his doctor to heal his condition, not permanently but for a brief period. No one wants to repeat the illness. Most doctors are forced to look away and use old phrases to describe the rest of us: "medicine is not omnipotent ...", "we do all we can to prevent it. ..." "I don't provide assurances, but I'll endeavor to assist you. ..." in these conversations patients are in awe: "How so? I require a complete outcome! Does it really seem impossible to be completely successful?"

A patient who is sick is looking for help, and requires it. He will seek out each expert's advice, go through lots of books and will search at everything that might aid him. Arguments in the manner of: "Well, okay, I'm an alcohol addict, let me alone." "maybe I'm seriously sick, or maybe I have to take a breather," the person is contradicting himself.

After recognizing that he's as sick, the person who is alcoholic transforms the issue from moral and ethics to medical. So, the question is: "And what if I am an alcoholicand I'm not drinking yet?" By itself, this is insignificant. Doctors are not lawyer and is not able to provide legal advice. Does it make sense to cough? Are you able to walk without an ache in your tooth? What if at holidays, I experience an outbreak of rash and a fever? Is it not possible?

All in all, against other forms of illnesses, the cure is based on you!

Chapter 3: Alter Your Way of Thinking

When confronted with any issue The first step in any situation is to acknowledge what's currently happening and acknowledge what the individual has done and is being doing at the moment.They must acknowledge that they've erred in drinking alcohol, and, in the process, have abused their use of alcohol which resulted in the abuse of alcohol and addiction.People need to recognize and accept what they've committed in the past in order that they can be able to know where they are now and what transpired because of the thing they've done.There is to be an determination to look at the current situation and also to believe to get to where they need to be or do what they are entitled to do.Without this step there would be no motivation to look at the present, which will hinder people from seeing their next possibility, in relation to their drinking alcohol intake.The first step is to establish a goal with rational thought and to realize that in consuming excessive amounts of alcohol, they've made an error that they must correct because it is unhealthy and unfit for them.As an expert on this field has stated the person will eventually end up in the wrong direction if he or she denies the problem, deflecting it and dismissing it as a minor issue. is not among the most crucial aspects that need to be changed in the course of life.

After a person has entered into a rational mind and has a clear mind, it is the time to recognize the purpose.They need to consider the reason they are doing this, or why they ought to consume a lot of alcohol for an unending time.What is the reason or goal behind the decision? Is there something positive that could gain from drinking excessively for a long period of time? Are there benefits? What are they? must try to meditate on the alcohol consumption which they are currently going through, and think about the benefits of this action bring to them as individuals. This is the ideal time to engage in contemplation, where the person begins to inquire about the purpose behind the actions are affected to.They must be aware that they don't simply drink because they're thirsty, but rather because of the impact of depression, anxiety, and pain.They are seeking something that will help them to get rid from the negative feelings, and have found their solution in drinking a glass of alcohol.Once they've recognized the reasons behind their actions they will understand the reason they're doing it and what they truly intend to achieve and whether they would like to keep doing it or eventually quit doing it.The motive will become clearer when they can comprehend the reason behind taking part in it.

Once the person has recognized the goal, it's the time to formulate the goal to stop the alcohol dependence once and all.They must choose to defeat the alcohol addiction.No one else can force the person to quit the alcohol addiction.It is their responsibility to decide whether they wish to keep going or would like to end it. They must realize the consequences of what they experience are all that they've hoped to occur to them.No person else will tell them to do this, to end this, or abandon this up.Even even if all their family members and acquaintances are there to help them abandon alcohol dependence all of them is useless until the individual decides to stop their own behavior, to take the initiative to do it themselves.If they don't choose to take action, there is no one who can do it for them.Thus it is up to them to make the choice to overcome addiction to alcohol. addiction.They must understand the reasons why they need to end the abuse of alcohol and then what they are likely to develop, as the result of drinking as well as addiction.As we have heard, the greatest influence in the lives of individuals is to be found in their minds and hearts of their minds.There is no one else that can take away these problems out of their lives, except their own and just them.

It is also important to imagine that the person they intend to become, they will in the near future become.It is crucial to understand the theory of expectation in which people believe that, what they desire to become will be what they eventually become.They must believe in this should they wish to get rid of the addiction and abuse of alcohol it will be a time when they can finally look back at these as incidents from the past.There is no longer drinking in their lives, but only the determination to do the steps necessary to stay in the right place - just enough for the moment and, for their body, and sufficient to feed the mind.If individuals have a certain expectation in their actions this goal can be accomplished with ease regardless of how difficult it may be for the moment being.In time they will be motivated to keep doing what they think they should do, because they are able to imagine themselves as light, that they are able to overcome the challenges of life, particularly in relation to alcoholism.The first step , therefore, is to focus their thoughts and minds and ensure that they're focused in completing their work regardless of how challenging it was at first.

Chapter 4: What is the reason We Drink

There will be a vast array of reasons that one might choose to drink. But there's a common tendency and some very general assertions that apply to the majority of, if not all alcohol drinkers in one way or other. This chapter will cover more than just the general motives that one might drink, but also the processes that take place within the human body and can impact the reason why someone drinks.

Genetics and Our Brains

The way that our genes work and how our brain works plays an important role in determining the reasons why people drink and also the likelihood of a person to develop into an alcohol addict. A few of the reasons our brain is involved will be discussed in the following portion of chapter.

In essence, our brains can are overwhelmed or overwhelmed due to a variety of reasons and want to get away from the stressor and to take a moment to settle itself. This is the point where alcohol can be found. It's not just an extremely easy method to relax because alcohol is often able to affect your thoughts in excessive quantities, causing the ability to temporarily forget what is in your mind and also, because it's a type of harm.

It might sound odd to say this however, there are times when people feel the need to harm themselves in one way or another to get themselves out of whatever state they're in, or to physically assure themselves that they are still alive. It's not happening in the same way as looking to relax or enjoy alcohol however it is possible when you plan to drink in order to be drunk. This isn't always the case however sometimes that's the way people feel about it.

There is also an increased desire to see drinking to relax when other members of our family have the same behavior. Different cultures have different views of alcohol and what is considered appropriate to drink, which means that drinking too much can be considered in different amounts depending on the country to country.

There are those who view drinking alcohol before 6 pm as an indication of being addicted and others believe that drinking at least a glass alcohol or wine at every meal is excessive. If you were raised in close relatives where your parents or other family members would pour out a glass of beers or wine when they were stressed and stressed, you'll inclined to try the exact things because you witnessed it regularly. It's an acceptable way to unwind and carry the concept until you're ready to drink yourself.

It can also make a difference whether there are alcohol and addicts within your familial lineage, or not. It might be more difficult to determine this when you're adopted however, it's something you need to be aware of, if it is possible. Being a parent of alcoholics can increases the chances of becoming an alcoholic later in your life. If you have family members who are addicts, it could increase the likelihood that you will become dependent on various substances, such as alcohol.

Being aware of your family's background, and knowing who you are, can aid you in understanding the ways alcoholism develops or better control how much you consume alcohol. Even if you're an alcohol user or recovering from an alcohol-related disorder, it's helpful to be aware of the facts. If you're already an alcohol user, it's already difficult to progress towards developing healthy habits. However, genetics can make it harder.

In any event, both your brain and genetics have a large impact on what you drink. Examine yourself - and possibly your family members too and determine if you are able to identify factors that may be the cause of your drinking. Being aware of you and your behavior will enable you to take a step closer to getting rid of your drinking habits since you'll be able to identify the areas to concentrate in the highest.

Common Reasons People Drink

There are a variety of factors that can lead a person to drink. The most popular reasons are:

Stress

Peer pressure

Social drinking (i.e. at a gathering with your friends)

Curiosity

The taste of alcohol

Are you in need of a boost to your confidence?

Accessibility for everyone

To appear older (if older than the age of legal)

Rebellion

An escape

In particular, for those experiencing extreme emotional stress it is likely that alcohol is an option they'll use. This is due to the fact that in a lot of societies, and especially Western society it is frequently portrayed in media as the most effective alternative when feeling pressured.

If you're not permitted to drink, lots of are compelled to drink due to the presence the presence of others drinking with them , or because they've been exposed to a variety of media that promotes drinking as a thing students in normal high schools or college students do on a daily basis. I'm not saying that it's uncommon for this to happen and is advertised by throwing a huge celebration at least once and drinking on almost every show geared towards those of the ages I've already discussed.

This notion is extensively promoted, even if it's trying to not present alcohol in a positive image - because alcohol is the most effective substance and method to improve the quality of life that a person is able to make use of. A few drinks occasionally isn't good however, having a constant drink or being totally drunk every time you drink isn't a good idea. If you do this, it will begin to put you in the direction of alcoholism when you are young.

The most important thing to remember away is to become aware of how much and the frequency with which you drink. This will allow you to be conscious of the possibility of having a problem should it arise and can enable you to stand up for yourself when you're getting pressured by your peers to take an alcohol drink, especially in the event that you hold to your beliefs.

Chapter 5: Dangers to Beware Of

It is vital to prepare yourself to drink fast.Not all people can quit cold turkey, so it's important to be aware and to have an action plan.We will outline an action plan in the next chapter of this book, but before that let's look at what could expect to happen.

Danger Signs Of Alcohol Detoxification

You might think that you're not a drinker because you only drink at weekends or take a drink every once or twice during the day.Your body could have other thoughts about this, and it is crucial that you keep an eye on the way your body functions while you are drinking alcohol fast.Alcohol withdrawal symptoms vary from moderate to serious; they can increase quickly , and have potentially deadly results.

Alcohol withdrawal is a real thing and can cause death to you.Everyone differs; although one person can be able to drink a few drinks for a day without becoming physically dependent of alcohol, another may not be as lucky.This is the reason you should be aware of the body's signals to you for the next six to 48 hours following the time the last time you drink.

I would recommend you don't do it alone.Have an individual you can trust around to help you through this time of need and inform them about the possible scenarios and how to manage it.

Social Drinker Vs. Addiction

I have always believed that I was a social drinker , so I thought I could either take it or take it or leave it.Addiction is a sneaky disease since it can sneak in on you.That is why the month-long detox to avoid alcohol important.If you are truly social drinker, then you will experience little to none effects of alcohol detox.However If you've been a victim of addiction to drinking, then the consequences of quitting "cold turkey" are more dramatic.Symptoms begin mild, but they will get more intense and eventually, you'll want to quit and have an alcohol drink to cause the symptoms to stop.This is a major warning sign that is a sign of an addiction.

My uncle drinks and doesn't exhibit any negative consequences from it.He appears to be the same regardless of regardless of whether or not he's drinking, and I don't believe I've ever witnessed his face drunk.My uncle has a hit-and miss drinker. He does not drink all day and certainly not every weekend.He might drink on an occasion or holiday occasion.I consider him to be as a social drinker, who, if he chose to cut down on drinking for a month, will be able to live with a few or none problems.His body's chemical makeup is such that alcohol doesn't bother him too much.

My mother and sister on the other side, can become drunk after only one drink.She is also a very low drinker at times, because she is aware that her tolerance to alcohol is terrible.She is an active drinker but is confined to drinking one drink at an event.My grandfather however, was a drinker all day long. However, he did not get drunk however, when he was forced to avoid drinking for reason of health, it turned out to be pure suffering through the detox process.

Since everyone reacts to alcohol in a different way and in a different way, it can be very difficult to know your own if you're an avid drinker or are dependent on alcohol.Here are some scenarios:

Let's imagine that your children who are between three and five play and Bobby becomes cranky, like many three-year-olds when they don't have their way or require an nap.Bobby begins crying because his brother is playing with a favourite toy but won't let him give the toy for him.A argument ensues and you need to end the fight and take your children for their rooms.You are in need of some alcohol to soothe your nerves.The children are calm in their rooms.You aren't usually drinking when things are chaotic, but however, this is the day. You pull out the vodka in the cupboard, add a tiny amount to an empty glass. You take a sip of it.That is it. You do not drink anything else, and you don't drink each time your children get into an argument. fight.If you are in this scenario, chances are you do not have any issues with alcohol.It is only problematic in the event that your spouse comes home at night to find you lying on the mattress in a drunken stupor.

In the second scenario the boss is accusing you of not performing your job correctly and not remembering to send in a report due days ago.You realize that you did not do the job you were supposed to do, and you blame it on every thing you can think of, even others co-workers.At lunchtime you are in a local bar, taking a drink to soothe your nerves, instead of having healthy meal.This was the 3rd time in the past week that you have visited the bar during lunch time, only to drink a glass of wine to cope with being unjustly treated at work.If you're in the same scenario, you may have an issue with drinking.You use alcohol as a coping mechanism and you blame everyone else for your mistakes.

While the two scenarios could each raise alarms, the mom who drinks only to soothe her anxiety is likely not addicted.She just wants an occasional drink, and she might or might not consume one.The person who has issues at work, who has been at the bar over the last four lunch hours is definitely suffering from problems.

The difference is in having a desire and needing an drink.If you are in the mood for a drink, but you are able to have it or quit, you don't have an addiction.If you are in the need of to drink after lunch each day due to pressures at work You should pay close careful attention to what you do since you may be dependent.

It is crucial to remember that alcohol of any kind is addictive.The person who consumes 10 beers every night is as dependent as the woman who pours down 3-4 glasses of wine each evening, or the guy who is at the bar to enjoy 8 shots of whiskey.It does not matter the type of drink you drink.You are equally addicted to alcohol by drinking fancy ice wine as you do with inexpensive Strawberry Hill.

Detox Signs to Watch

As I mentioned earlier there is a chance that you will not suffer any withdrawal symptoms due to alcohol.Your symptoms could be mild and inconsequential.This could suggest that you are truly a drinker in a social setting and does not suffer from addiction.

My father was the first to know about addiction.His dad was an alcohol addict, so because of that, along with the fact that some of his brothers also were dependent on alcohol, he was able to avoid it.I believe he had one or two drinks per year around New Years Eve and Christmas Eve. If he had decided to completely abstain from alcohol and never drink again, he'd have suffered minimally.

His sister drank several drinks every weekend.Once she noticed that she was gaining weight and she made the decision to stop.She suffered from minimal symptoms, and the withdrawal process didn't bother the woman much.Another brother was a frequent drinker who, due to legal problems was forced to enter recovery.He had withdrawal symptoms such that he was forced to be hospitalized.So it is evident that the severity of the adverse effects of alcohol on you will be determined by the amount you drink and your metabolism.

Withdrawal

The withdrawal symptoms typically begin to manifest around six to eight hours after having had your last drink, however, they may appear at any time, as little as 2 hours later.Withdrawal symptoms occur at their highest within 24 to 48 hours following the last drink, and disappear in between five and seven days.The below are the signs you must be aware of:

Drink cravings can become intense after a couple of hours of being without anything.Try to keep yourself away from your cravings as best as you can by drinking soft drinks or even water with a bit of citrus added.Ice tea can be refreshing and it is also a great source of caffeine.

Tremors in legs and hands also known as delirium or DTs and can be mild or serious.Most people have DTs as a result of withdrawal from alcohol but they are rarely severe.They could be fatal however, and are not something to play with.During DTs you may feel frustrated, angry, confused depressed or anxious and may have nightmares.You may experience headache nausea, vomiting and headache and may sweat profusely.This is among the first signs of withdrawal to show.

Falls are common when detoxing, mainly due to the destabilizing effects of DTs.That is another reason to need someone to monitor your progress during this time.

It is common for people to experience dehydration in withdrawal, mostly due to it's extremely difficult for the stomach to endure even water.However it is important to remain hydrated.Water is the best option however it can be difficult to swallow.Fizzy water can alleviate stomach upset at the very least little.If you suspect that your dehydration is severe and you're unable to stop vomiting, it's ideal to seek out an emergency room.You are not failing in the event that you require medical assistance but you need help.Do not be afraid to seek assistance when you require it.It is much better to seek assistance than die.

The hallucinations can occur between 12-24 hours into the withdrawal.This is another reason to should have someone with you throughout detoxification.The hallucinations could be quite mild.You may find yourself at the front of the refrigerator and you don't know what you did to get there or the reason you're there.You might also experience unpleasant hallucinations, and you feel like that your existence is danger.Severe hallucinations are not something to play with.They can be a valid reason to seek out an emergency department.

Seizures can occur within 24 to 48 hours after detoxification.About 2 to 3 percent people who undergo detox suffer seizures of some kind that is often caused due to dehydration.Seizures can be characterized by convulsions or being thrown down, however they can be as simple as staring at space or in a state of not being able to respond to stimuli. If you experience convulsions, the person who is with you should seek urgent help.The most effective thing that a person who is helping is able to do when you're in convulsions is to help you roll on your back and remain in the room, stopping you from hitting anything that could cause injury to the person.

Go to The Hospital

If you are experiencing any of the symptoms listed below Be safe and go to the hospital

*Temperature above 101 degrees Fahrenheit

If your pulse is at 115 or greater is a good indication to download an alarm for pulse rate to your smartphone. phone.They perform pretty well.

*Systolic blood pressure that is 170 or greater.

• Dehydration that is severe. capable of sustaining a steady level for more than eight hours.

*Convulsive seizures.

Hallucinations that are uncontrollable.

Do not risk the possibility that you could be hurt by any of these.

I'm not trying make you feel uncomfortable during your abstinence for a month, however it would have been remiss of me if didn't let you know what can happen during an alcohol detox.I am sure I don't want injury to anyone one of my followers.

In the majority of cases your symptoms won't be extreme; mine were not all that bad.I was afflicted with DTs for a few days, However, they were tolerable.I didn't experience hallucinations or seizures, high temperatures, or heart racing problems.My thirst for alcohol was quite intense, however, I had a person to distract me from it all times.

The feeling of detoxing can be uneasy But keep in mind that nothing worthwhile ever is cheap.You can try it; you'll be grateful later in the event that you do not.

Be prepared so that nothing is unexpected surprise.This involves examining methods for sobriety.There are numerous options to pick, and you can test one or the combination of several.We will examine the various methods we have explored within the sections that follow.This will give you guidance in creating your own personal plan for quitting drinking.

It is crucial to know the possibilities of what can happen.You could be one of those lucky people who experience absolutely no problems However your body may react to the process of detoxification in many ways.It's crucial to be aware of the warning signs and seek help promptly should it be necessary.Detox symptoms can quickly escalate and can have fatal results.Don't be one of the statistic.You would like to be able to have fun with your family, your friends and life for the rest of your.

Why do we do bizarre things when we drink alcohol?

This is among the most important factors that help those around us to be aware of when we drink. One of the most important elements of alcohol that make it attractive to the masses is that it acts as an invigorating drink and it can help lessen our inhibitions. However, this positive aspect of alcohol can also be a huge negative. The people who drink aren't themselves when they drink, and are often prone to do or do things not in line with their character. While the behavior is bizarre, it can also be harmful and even dangerous.

Maybe that lack of self-control could be the reason people drink and continue to do so. The feeling that you can speak or act anything and not look stupid is enough of as a reason to drink more often and feel more confident in a social setting.

After having a few drinks, and inhibitions quickly disappearing the drinkers are more talkative in a row, be more raunchy, and generally behave in a different way from normal. Then they will experience the sensation of being "high'. It is not true that they are experiencing a high, but rather the nervous system of their body is slowing down.

The first few days are the "stuff that people will remember" the most in their hearts. There are a few drinks and you feel more confident, more socially competent, and more able to be a more confident extrovert. The first consequences of alcohol are:

*Relaxation

An increased feeling of wellbeing

*Low alertness

*Lack of inhibition

* A feeling of happiness

And all of these result from just a couple of beers.

Since our nerves are directly affected by alcohol, and it's initially such an enjoyable experience that we drink until we reach late stages of intoxication when we begin to stumble around, begin to lose our control over our thoughts and actions.

This could lead to embarrassing situations in which our behavior becomes unbearable and we begin to act in ways that others wouldn't want us to.

If we travel through the city streets at night and spot those who have drank often, it would not be unusual to see the people crying, running around in a convulsive manner or arguing, and even undressed. All of this behavior is directly attributed to drinking excessively.

Our behavior is this way because one of the major negative effects that alcohol has on the bodies is the lack of inhibition. This is the norm. Humans are prone to believe that they're free from inhibitions even if it's just for a few hours. They then behave according to their beliefs.

Do we need to drink alcohol during medication?

There are many out there who claim that drinking alcohol while taking medications is very risky. It is true, especially in the event that you drink heavily while taking medications.

In reality, doctors advise us to avoid drinking while taking medication. They do not really tell us the reason, but they do inform us to drink.

What is the reason you think they're doing this? They do this because they do not want alcohol to hinder the effectiveness of the drug. There is no doubt that with certain drugs you should not drink, however with most drugs, it's quite safe to drink moderately.

Since the alcohol in your system is depressant it alters how your brain functions. Because many drugs are depressants, or possess effects that are sedative, they alter the way your brain functions too.

It could indicate that you have two chemicals in your body that reduce the brain's ability to react to alarm signals about danger, or even think in a positive way.

It could also mean that alcohol has the ability to reduce the effect of the substances you're taking. It may lessen the effects and, consequently, alter the time to recover that you would have desired. Alcohol also has such negative effects on the drug that it has a negative impact on your health.

It's a lot more hazardous when you use medications that are intended to aid you in sleeping or calm. The effects of alcohol and the sedative you've consumed can make you more drowsy and expose you to serious risk.

In the case of antibiotics, the scenario differs. Certain antibiotics, when combined in conjunction with alcohol, may cause various side effects that are present. Certain antibiotics with alcohol component can cause flushing and nausea for instance.

Certain conditions can cause an increase in heart rate and breathlessness. If you have a heart disease or suffer from asthma, these issues are likely to get worse and may even lead to death.

In the case of drinking or taking medications, make sure to consult with your doctor before you drink. They are the best. If they advise against drink, then don't.

Chapter 6: The Effects of Alcoholism explained

Alcoholism is the most severe form of drinking-related disorder. It includes all the indicators of alcohol addiction however there is an additional element that is crucial. This is the physical dependence of alcohol. If you depend on it to function , or think you must drink to keep alive You're probably an alcoholic.

A few of the symptoms of an alcoholic are:

Tolerance. It is necessary to drink increasing amounts to feel relaxed and to get buzz. You consume more than the average and you do not get drunk. These are all indications of tolerance to alcohol and is the first indication of alcohol dependence. Tolerance implies that you require increasing amounts of alcohol to experience the same sensation of buzzing.

Withdrawal. If you are forced to drink to maintain your hands shaking early in the morning or drink to alleviate or prevent experiencing withdrawal symptoms, it's warning signs. When you drink heavily the body will learn to accept the alcohol and then you start to experience the withdrawal symptoms listed below as you attempt to quit:

Afraid and jumpiness

Sweating

A trembling

Nausea or vomiting

Depression

Insomnia

Fatigue

Irritability

Headache

Appetite loss

In extreme cases, it could result in hallucinations, confusion, seizures, fever, and disturbance.

You've lost control over your drinking. You are no longer able to consume as much alcohol as you desire, but you have to continue drinking. You consume more alcohol than you think you will even though you say you won't.

You'd like to quit but aren't able to. You're determined to give up, but you haven't been able to build the motivation to actually quit.

You have given up other pursuits in the pursuit of drinking. You are spending lesser and less socializing with friends or family members and exercising, or engaging in hobbies, and spend more time in the bar.

Alcohol requires an enormous amount of focus and energy. You're likely to spend the majority of your time contemplating drinking or drinking, as well as recovering from having a drink. There are very few social activities or interests which don't revolve around drinking drinks.

You consume alcohol even when you are aware that it is causing problems. It's possible that you're making your relationships less enjoyable, causing health issues or causing depression to worsen however, you keep drinking.

The biggest obstacle is denial. for alcoholics to seek assistance. The urge to drink is so powerful to drink that the brain keeps trying to justify the drinking even though the negative consequences are clear. If you don't look seriously at your actions and actions, you can create more issues that arise with work, finances and relationships.

Denial comes in various forms, but here are the most often seen

Don't overestimate how much you drink

To reduce the bad effects of drinking

The idea that family and friends are exaggerating

The blame game for drinking problems is often blamed on other people.

You could accuse your manager of problems at work, or your irritable wife for marital problems. While stress from work, financial and relationship issues are common to all people, the general pattern of degrading and blame can indicate trouble.

If you are able to justification your drinking, make up excuses about them, or are unable to discuss the issue, take a moment to examine the reasons you feel like you're so defensive. If you think you're not in trouble There shouldn't be any reason the reason you're hiding your drinking or trying to justify your drinking.

The five myths alcohol addicts often tell themselves.

I'm able to quit drinking if I wish to. You may be able to do so, however, the most likely scenario is that you aren't able to. It's another reason to keep drinking. In reality, you're not ready to quit. If you tell yourself that you are able to quit this makes you feel as though you're in charge despite all evidence to the contrary and you're not concerned about the harm it's causing.

The drinking is my issue and I'm the one who is hurting; therefore, no one else is entitled to demand that I stop. The decision to quit drinking is completely yours but you're deceiving yourself if you think your drinking doesn't hurt anyone else than you. The effects of alcohol affect everyone around you, including our family and friends. This is their problem as well.

I don't drink daily and therefore, I'm not an drinker. I enjoy drinking beer or wine but I'm not an alcohol-dependent. Alcoholism doesn't define it by how often you drink, the type of drink you consume or the amount you consume. It's the consequences of your drinking that determine the issue. If your drinking creates anxiety or causes problems at home, at work or school and you are an issue. It doesn't matter if have a drink on weekends only or consume only wine or beer. There's a problem everywhere.

I'm not a alcoholic just because I'm employed. Alcoholism doesn't depend on the fact that you're employed or are homeless. Many alcoholics manage to complete their education as well as work and support their families. Some are successful in their alcohol-related phases. However, just because you are able to perform well on alcohol does not mean you're not placing others or yourself at risk.

Alcohol consumption isn't a true addiction, like addiction to drugs. Contrary to what many believe that alcohol is a substance and is just as detrimental to the human body and psyche like other substances. It can cause changes in the brain as well as the body, and over time, abuse can be detrimental to your job, health and relationships as any other substance.

Alcoholism can affect every aspect that you live. A long-term addiction can lead to grave health issues, and damage the majority of organs in the body including your brain, and cause emotional harm, too. It could cause issues with your finances, career and the ability to keep good relationships. Alcoholism can affect your colleagues along with your family members and even your close friends.

If you're ready to admit you have an alcohol issue and you've made that first step. It requires a lot of determination and courage to admit that you are an alcohol addict. The second step is to seek out support. the next step.

Chapter 7: Signs of Alcoholism

The alcohol-related habits can be difficult to identify, but unlike heroin or cocaine, but alcohol is easily accessible and it is a common practice in various societies. It's usually the foundation of relationships between people and is usually associated to celebrations and enjoyment.

Drinking alcohol is an integral aspect of some lives For others they are influenced by the culture, but it's difficult to distinguish between those who drink often and those who are addicted to it.

The signs of addiction to alcohol include:

Increase in the amount of intake.

Alcohol tolerance is high.

Alcohol consumption at inappropriate times and in inappropriate places.

Looking to be in the place an area where lots of alcohol is e.g at a gathering, party, etc.

Change in friendship: Someone who enjoys drinking may pick those who consume a lot of alcohol.

Avoiding contact in family relationships.

Denying and hiding the fact the fact that you have drank alcohol.

Dependent on alcohol to do work or participate in the activities.

Legal or professional issues, like arrests or loss of an employment.

When addiction becomes more severe after a time it is important to recognize the early symptoms of addiction (if diagnosed and treated quickly) Someone who is who is addicted to alcohol would likely not acknowledge the signs.

If you're concerned about one of your friends is dependent on alcohol, try not to make them feel ashamed and making them feel guilt-ridden. This could make them withdraw or cause them to be resistant to your help, instead be encouraging and reassuring them.

Medical Conditions Related to alcoholism

The addiction to alcohol can cause liver and coronary heart diseases, and it could result in:

Ulcer.

Diabetes.

Sexual issues.

Congenital disabilities.

Bone loss.

Eye problems.

Cancer risk is higher.

Supressed immune function.

A person who is addicted to alcohol could risk others' lives due to their insidious state. Based on the statistics of the Centres for Disease Control and Avoidance (CDC) around 28,000 individuals in the U.S have been killed as a result of suicide and homicide. It is believed that this is mostly due to alcoholism.

This is a good reason the need to tackle alcohol dependence early. The majority of the issues associated with drinking addiction could be prevented or dealt with through long-term recovery.

Treatment Options for alcoholism?

The treatment for addiction to alcohol can be difficult and complex. In order for treatment to be effective for the patient suffering from an addiction must abstain from drinking the alcohol they can or cut down on their intake. You shouldn't try to force them to not drink when they're not prepared. Treatment success is dependent on the individual's determination to get better.

The process of healing from alcoholism may require an ongoing commitment. There isn't a quick solution that is not a continuous maintenance; because of this, many believe that people suffering from alcoholism do not ever "healed."

Rehabilitation

The most commonly used treatment option for people suffering from alcohol dependence is either inpatient or outpatient program. A program for inpatients could last for anywhere from 30 days to a year; it typically reduces the symptoms of drawback as well as psychological problems. Outpatient therapy provides continuous support and allows patients to return home.

Alcoholics Anonymous and other Organizations

People who are dependent on alcohol and require help might want to look into the 12-step model similar to Alcoholics Anonymous (AA); Some organizations don't adhere to the 12-step format but prefer Wise Recovery as well as Sober Recovery.

No matter what support system you choose the support system is, it's important to try to remain sober. It can help those struggling with the addiction to alcohol. A welcoming atmosphere can provide real-life experiences and solid and healthy assistance; These things can help an addict and give them a an environment that is comfortable in the event of an occurrence of return.

Other Options Someone suffering from an alcohol dependence may also benefit from advantages of a variety of treatment options, including:

Drug therapy.

Counseling.

Food-related changes.

Doctors can prescribe medications to treat specific conditions, e.g, antidepressants. Antidepressants are effective if the person who is addicted to alcohol is taking self-medication for his/her depression or when doctors prescribe medication to deal in other issues that can be related to recovery.

It is simple to go to sessions with a therapist to educate one with the best ways to reduce the risk of strain during recovery and to stay away from any return. In addition, healthy eating could assist in repairing the harm drinking alcohol has done to one's health such as regaining weight.

Treatment for alcohol dependence may require different treatment strategies. The addict must enroll in one of these programs that can help support the long-term recovery process; it could be a therapeutic session for someone who suffers from depression.

Where can one get help in the fight against alcohol dependence?

To learn more about alcoholism, or to help those you love to help them It is recommended to consult a physician. They may refer you to local programs, like centres or the 12 Step program. Additionally, the following organizations may be helpful:

National Council on Alcoholism and Medication Dependence (NCADD).

National Institute on Alcohol consumption Abuse and Alcoholism (NIAAA).

National Institute on Drug abuse.

The drug abuse industry and the Mental Health Services Administration.

What's the view on alcoholism?

Treatment for alcohol dependence early is recommended since addictions that last longer are harder to conquer but the most effective treatment is designed to help long-term habitual behavior.

Families and friends of those who suffer from addiction to alcohol can assist them in getting professional assistance or enroll in programs such as Al-Anon.

An individual suffering from addiction to alcohol who has been sober for several weeks or years may be able to recognize that they're experiencing an episode of relapse. This may be the result of excessive drinking. In the end, sobriety could be the responsibility of any person affected by alcohol. It is crucial to avoid encouraging harmful behaviours and to keep reasonable limits if an addicted person continues to drink. it could mean removing funding if it is going to cause them to be unable to satisfy their desire.

If you know someone who is addicted, try to encourage them and offer emotional assistance.

Chapter 8: Health Damages Due To Alcohol Consumption

Alcohol is seen as an alcohol drink that is social and means of connecting with others. It is a way to celebrate successes and is popular at social occasions. Personally the majority of people drink alcohol simply because they enjoy it or when they're depressed. This is where the problem lies. Drinking alcohol isn't considered to be a serious matter. A pint here, a shot there, or a glass of wine isn't a huge deal...that is how it begins and you don't even realize it until the damage has been done. It is when you become addicted to alcohol and experience withdrawal symptoms if you do not drink. This is the thing you have to be aware of when you decide to avoid alcohol and you are in a better position that those who don't.

Common Health Detriments

It is not an innocuous drink or beverage since in medical terms it's classified as an "depressant." This signifies that alcohol slows essential body functions, resulting with blurred vision erratic movement along with slurred speech. It also can make it difficult to think rapidly. Whatever the amount of consumption is, alcohol affects your brain severely. Alcohol is a substance that can negatively affect a person's mental faculties and can alter one's judgement. It is difficult to think clearly in the event that you frequently drink alcohol.

Alcohol Overdose

It's not a good idea to consume it in small amounts therefore how can one expect to avoid harm when taken in huge amounts? If it's consumed in quantities that the body isn't able to manage, the effects of alcohol's depressant can be felt by the drinker. They lose their coordination and control and feel the "dumb feel". Alcohol Poisoning is more hazardous because it triggers more extreme depressant effects. This includes:

Inability to feel the pain

The poison is extremely toxic and is eliminated from the body

Unconsciousness

In worst cases, coma or death

How Alcohol harms the body

Understanding the process of science through how alcohol impacts the body can help you understand the harm it can cause. It is absorbed into bloodstream via small blood vessels that line the lining of the stomach and the small in the intestine. It's fast and travels from the stomach to the brain in just a few minutes of drinking. It rapidly affects nerve cells and reduces their functioning. 20 percent of the alcohol passes via the stomach, while the remainder is absorbed via the small intestinal tract. It is then transported to the liver where it is "metabolized" to a non-toxic substance. But, only a small amount of it is metabolized, and the excess goes throughout the body, causing negative effects and accumulating toxic substances within the body. The severity of the impacts is determined by the amount consumed. When it comes to alcohol Poisoning the respiratory system is slowed down enough that it could lead to an involuntary coma or even death due to the fact that oxygen is not able to get to the brain.

Alcohol can harm every organ of the body including important organs and system. They include:

Pancreas and Liver

They are the organs responsible for the processing of metabolic waste products that our body produces. In general, pancreas and gallbladder perform their work to assist digestion and absorption of nutrients. The pancreas releases enzymes, while the gallbladder releases bile. Both of which work together to digest food.

Pancreas regulates insulin as well and helps maintain blood glucose levels.

When someone drinks an alcohol drink, their pancreas creates toxic substances that can disrupt its normal functioning, resulting in inflammation. This is known as pancreatitis. This condition can damage the pancreas.

The liver is a key part of the metabolism, and also in removing the toxic substances by breaking them down into non-harmful substances. As alcohol is known to be a toxic substance that is why it is taken to the liver for being reduced into a harmless substance. Alcohol consumption that is excessive may "overload" the liver, which can lead to alcohol-related Hepatitis. Hepatitis is a form of liver inflammation. This can lead to an additional dangerous condition known as the cirrhosis which causes severe scarring to the liver. It could lead to organ failure too as potentially life-threatening. Drinking alcohol can cause liver cancer.

If the liver and pancreas fail to function as they should this causes problems with insulin levels and blood glucose levels. Blood glucose levels is high or high. This is why alcohol is extremely harmful to diabetics.

Nervous System

Alcohol is easily absorbed by the body and enters the nervous system where it may have negative consequences. It alters your behaviour, making it difficult to speak and alters your control and coordination. If someone drinks excessively is it hard to concentrate and can cause a risk to their ability to control their impulses and the brain area which controls memory.

In the long term drinking may cause a shrinkage in the frontal lobes of the brain. This causes permanent brain damage and leads to dementia. If the nervous system gets affected in this manner this causes numbness discomfort or "weird sensations" on the feet and hands. Alcohol consumption can cause your vitamin B1 levels to drop which could have a adverse affect upon your vision.

In addition to these issues, when alcohol dependence becomes a problem it can be difficult to quit it all at once in the same way as other kinds of addictions, withdrawal from alcohol can life-threatening. When you are experiencing withdrawal symptoms, they include nausea as well as anxiety, shaking, and anxiety. In the most severe instances it can cause hallucinations and seizures. This type of dependency is treated only by medical professionals via medical detoxification.

Digestive System

Alcohol actually "tortures" the digestive system. From the mouth to the colon alcohol can be extremely damaging to your colon. The abuse of alcohol can cause gum tooth decay and gum disease. Drinking heavily can cause the development from ulcers inside the esophagus or stomach. Additionally, it can trigger problems such as heartburn and acid reflux.

The inflammation of the pancreas can affect the digestive system and impacts the stomach's capacity to digest food and regulate metabolism. The damage can cause diarrhoea, abdominal fullness and gassiness. The effects of drinking too much can be life-threatening, as it could cause internal bleeding.

People who drink are malnourished as alcohol can make it difficult for the digestive tract to absorb the necessary nutrients, vitamins , and to control bacteria. This can lead to neutralization of the food supplements you take.

The most serious illness that alcohol causes is cancer. It is not just the cause of liver cancer, but can also be responsible for the development of mouth throat, throat, esophagus or colon cancer.

Circulatory System

The heart is also affected severely by alcohol consumption. Women are at greater chance of suffering from heart problems when compared to males. The risk to the circulation system include:

Unusual heartbeat

Heart muscles that have been pounded

Stroke

High blood pressure

Angina

Heart attack

Immune System

Due to all the harms that alcohol can cause to your body, it's recognized that alcohol weakens the immune system. This causes problems in combating viruses, germs and various illnesses. People who drink are more susceptible to ailments such as TB as well as pneumonia. There is a greater chance of developing different types of cancer among heavy drinkers.

If it is clear that alcohol is not beneficial and is not beneficial, it's a good idea to cut down on drinking. This will not only enhance your overall health, but it will also allow you be more positive and create positive modifications to your lifestyle.

Chapter 9: Tell Your Family And Friends

If you're not sure you want to be quiet about stopping drinking, I suggest first talking to your family members or acquaintances. If you're in good standing with them, there's an opportunity that they'll be happy with your decision, and will display an interest in your progress. It is always beneficial to know there are people in your life who are supportive and following your advancement. If you tell someone about your goals, you're planting an idea in your brain. If your goal is put out there and everyone knows about it, it's likely you'll put in the effort to getting it done because you realize that others follow your progress, you're determined to show them that you are capable of doing it. So if you want to give up in a day, or a month, or in the course of a year, inform them that you will achieve it.

Keep in mind that at times there is this one boring aunt who loves to criticize our actions. We all have him. He's unhappy about his life or circumstances, and therefore he is determined to drag those around him down by dragging them down. If that is the case, in the crowd in your vicinity, I'd advise against speaking to him or others who are near to him. Pick your closest friends. There is no need for negative influences within your daily life. It's impossible to change the behavior of others. behavior , therefore in my opinion that it is better to leave those individuals in peace and refrain from communicating my plans with them.

Be aware that even though your family members and friends may understand the situation, others will not. They may not be aware of the severity of your problem because you haven't yet been admitted to a hospital or suffered several serious issues arising from your drinking. It's possible that you've been competent in keeping your drinking secret from your friends and family members, but it could be an enormous surprise to some of them when you step out of the closet and reveal drinking.

Keep your faith in the Lord

It is important to build your self-confidence and believe that you are capable of doing this. It is not necessary to tear yourself down. You must be your own friend , too. Know that you have control over your actions during this life. It's not the alcohol. Certain programs want you to believe that you're completely powerless. I'm not saying that! You're not a shell just waiting to get filled with any program or god who will offer a solution for you. It is vital to avoid falling into the trap of thinking that you are an alcohol addict and feeling powerless. In doing so, you're creating a greater risk to it.

Begin to see yourself as a wonderful person. A winner is not a loser. Have you heard of the expression "Fake it until You

Make the Mistake"?. While I'm certainly not one to believe in falsehoods, fake news, or deceiving people, I believe that if you repeat something repeatedly, it will start manifesting within your head. Even if you're not a successful person or think you're not very proud of yourself, begin to tell yourself that you are not. I am sure. It's absurd. If you start each day in front of your mirror, and tell yourself "I'm an amazing, caring fascinating, interesting and fun person that deserves all the wonderful things the world can give!" you will start to believe in yourself more and feel more relaxed. You will also have more confidence. Why? The power of words is evident. You've probably had the experience of someone saying something negative to you, don't you think? Did it cause pain? It surely did. There are feelings. However, if someone came up directly to you with the wordsto you "Wow you're awesome!" - you would feel great, wouldn't you? The act of saying it to yourself has the same effect.

Begin to build your confidence as it will help you in facing any obstacles that may be encountered while you work towards becoming clean. Be positive, stay motivated and believe that you are going to win. Take self-strengthening classes and learn new things. change your clothes change your hairstyle, and alter your lifestyle. You're no more the same person that you was. The goal of quitting drinking is the best way to change your life, so why not take it to the end of the road and begin your new life? It's still going to be who you are obviously. However, you'll be leaving your history, your bad habits as well as your bad life style with the other bad things that have defined your life up to now. It's not a big deal to alter your hairstyle, however for a lot of people it can be an extremely physically and a big declaration for others to know that they've made a new beginning and are determined to make a change to become a better person. For some , this may seem like an insignificant thing, but when you put these small pieces together and begin making your selections, they will begin to create an entirely new person. You'll begin to feel as if you're a different person and those who are around you will start to take notice and become interested in what you're doing. It's all about beginning with a small amount. We're building a new future we wish to be able to endure, isn't a quick fix which will become overwhelming after just two weeks. Therefore, by gradually introducing the new ideas in your life, you'll be able to adjust to the changes as well as a new life , and to a better future.

Find alternative options

Many people who are drinking alcohol for a long period, some do not know how to spend their spare time after they've decided to end their drinking. If they've been drinking for a long period of time or spent time in bars (which is usually their sole source of socializing) or in the company of fellow drinkers , it might be difficult to be forced to make a choice. For those who do not suffer from an addiction or abuse of alcohol, it's not an issue to arrange their time. For those with alcohol addiction, it's difficult. Therefore, I strongly suggest seeking the help of a group of individuals who are in the same position as you. A lot of people who suffer from alcohol issues don't have families nor many friends. A large number of people have abandoned their addiction and aren't interested in to be in contact due to their struggles. A support group could prove very beneficial. It's not just a means of helping people who struggle to quit drinking to drink, but also an opportunity to enjoy your spare time. Consider it as a substitute for drinking at the bar. Instead of filling up your body up with toxic liquids, you're filling it with knowledge, support and love from people around you.

The research also shows that after quitting drinking, particularly when you've been drinking for a long period individuals still experience the desire to feel as if they are drinking liquids by mouth. Around 90% of those who stop drinking alcohol switch towards coffee to satisfy the craving. Research isn't clear if this being a good or negative thing, however in comparison to those who do not have issues with alcohol, less than 50% consume the same amount of coffee (up to 5 cups per day) like those who recently quit drinking alcohol. I'm a big coffee drinker, and I think it's good for my health. Sure , it's stimulating but my personal opinion is that it helps me be more active as I feel like I would like to get out and get involved in activities and also helps me get up to get up in the morning.

I have heard of a few individuals who were able to switch to other alcoholic drinks such as coctails and beers, and continue to go to bars and restaurants that serve them . They are fine with that and remain sober. However, for those who are looking to stop drinking and remain sober, this could be a hazardous situation, and my view is that it must be avoided. If you are looking to remain sober, alter your life and habits, I suggest staying clear of bars and nightclubs. Particularly at the beginning.

It's possible that you will feel at ease for certain locations without feeling the need to drink alcohol, but when you're getting into your rhythm in, changing your lifestyle and sanitizing your life, I do not see the value of visiting these venues. There are alternatives to get together with your friends, if that's the thing you're looking for and if they're the only places where you get to meet them, is it worth the effort? It wasn't for me.

There were a group of friends I only saw at bars while drinking. I thought to myself "what do I gain from this?" What is the value of friendship one that only exists in the moment you're drinking? What value is it bringing to you? Do you really want to be having this relationship? If you're asking you this same question, and the answer is yes , it is possible that you must decide and put up some sacrifices. Everyone has to make certain sacrifices in the course of our lives. It's the way things are. There is no guarantee that life will be easy or that progress could be effortless.

Nobody has said that quitting using alcohol will be easy.

You might be thinking "why do I have to stop a friendship in order to stop drinking? Can't I do each?". It's not my intention to provide a definitive answer to this. It's up to yourself the question and then be honest. Does this friendship benefit me? Which is more important? My decision and decision on abstinence from drinking or my previous friends? It is better to stay far from these areas and seek out other activities which help you grow as an individual. Join a group, go for walks in nature, visit an exhibition of art (they typically aren't expensive) and, if you are interested in an interest, and take a class, and learn something new. Choose to live an enjoyable life, free of the need to consume pollutants. Once you've made that decision, you will begin to notice improvements. If you share positive experiences, you will be rewarded. Stop living the same way and begin a fresh one, with new ways of living. If you're stuck in the same way and aren't doing anything, you shouldn't expect that things will be different for you. Therefore, just do it.

Chapter 10: Benefits of Quitting

Most of us find that drinking alcohol can be a delightful moment. If you sip a glass of alcohol or 16oz of beer, and enjoy the flavor, you know the company you're spending the cash with and let's face it , the outcomes from a couple of glasses are pretty good as well. That's one reason to avoid drinking alcohol, however for a mere month may be a bit shaky as it's taking away the pleasure that we get from it.

Reading this section is the first step in making changes and ensuring the best month of your life. When it comes to making any improvements in your life and avoiding something we love, the most way to stay motivated is to outline the advantages you'll reap by changing your lifestyle. But in order to achieve this, you must know the nature of these benefits. It is true that alcohol is vital for researchers, and numerous people have done their research to help you.

In 2013, an audience of 10 curious columnists from The UK's New Researcher magazine chose to cut down on drinking for a month , and analyze the effects on their bodies. They convinced a number of doctors from University College London Medical School and the London's Royal Free Hospital ready. The doctors created a sequence of estimations based on benchmarks before the columnists began their tests. At the end of the month, the participants had lost weight and had lowered their cholesterol and their livers were much healthier state than when the month began.

Incredulous, the scientists decided to repeat the test with a larger number of people.

The group of 10 people grew to 104 persons aged over 40 who had decided to stay clear of drinking alcohol in January. In general, prior to the first meeting, women were having a drink of 29 units in seven days (almost three bottles of beer or fourteen pints) as well as the males had consumed 31 units of alcohol, enough to be classified as heavy drinkers. In any event, within around a month of not drinking their livers, they began to heal themselves, and various aspects of their wellbeing, including the strain on their circulatory system in addition to their susceptibility to hormones like insulin, had improved. There were also some evident immediate physical benefits, such as better sleep and concentration.

This may be enough for some to make the decision to test right here, currently however if you require more details, keep reading and I'll talk about in depth the six major regions as well as the wealth of advantages that you will gain in the event that you quit drinking alcohol for a whole month.

The act of quitting can affect your health and well-being.

Although it's true that in small amounts alcohol has benefits for health, it's not recommended to consume more than amounts, and the impacts on your body can be harmful. The process of reducing is much as if you're sending your body to occasion to give it a break from something that could be causing anxiety. In this way you'll start to experience some evident positive results within a couple time of a long period of surrender.

Your Vitality and Rest Enhance

The findings were echoed by participants from both preliminary studies. The researchers revealing that restraint increased the rest of people by 10. The reason for this is simple alcohol negatively affects your sleep. It's not the first time, at first it acts as an invigorating and soothing experience that causes you to fall asleep quickly and this is the reason that many people use alcohol as a way to end their night. When you've sunk the world changes. In the beginning, alcohol blocks your body from moving through sleep phases in the same way you normally be, and it triggers more restlessness throughout the rest in the evening. In addition researchers from Australia have discovered that mind's waves change the post-alcohol sleep. Instead of just creating tranquil delta waves that are associated with relaxation and rest it also produces alpha waves that aren't usually noticed as we fall asleep. Scientists say that the double wave process can confuse the mind and lead to an insufficient amount of rest . The result is that no matter if you sleep through the night, you're more likely to suffer from daytime fatigue migraines, a lowered mood the next day.

However, it's highly unlikely that you'll sleep between sunset and sundown. Typically, the process of peeing shuts at night to allow us to sleep all day long. However alcohol is a diuretic and alters this process to its importance; you're more likely to have to get up to go to the bathroom. Alcohol can also cause us to breathe more easily by loosing the tissues in the throat that then vibrate when we breathe in. And If there's something that is guaranteed to wake you up that's the burrowing elbow of your companion who's unable to rest due to you making them aware. Sleepwalking as well as bad dreams are more likely when you've had a drink.

Stop drinking and it happens very rapidly All things considered for those who are generally mild drinkers sleep, better rest - and the your vitality that follows it - are the main advantages you'll experience during your vacation.

Your Liver Recovers

Although changes in the quality of your sleep and energy are obvious physical signs that you feel, the things are also changing within your body on an individual level after you stop.

They're not as easy to recognize but you can be sure you can detect them particularly within your liver.

It is the primary organ in the body that produces alcohol. A risk associated with drinking too much is the growth of fat in the liver while it processes this. These fat cells release an inflammatory mix, which could damage the cells surrounding them. Alcohol can also harm the covering of your digestive tract which allows intestinal microorganisms to get into the circulatory system. If they reach the liver area, they could cause damage to the cells. These kinds of injuries may cause scarring to the liver, which from the beginning can be reversed; however should you continue to attack the liver, you'll create permanent scarring in the liver, which will eventually alter its capabilities - an illness called cirrhosis.

The risk of having a the liver becoming fatty for men who consume more than 8 units per day for a half-month For women it is just five units per day during the same time frame to develop symptoms. Most likely, you're not likely to be aware of this, however, since the majority of the damage to your liver doesn't show any visible signs.

Get a break then the liver is able to repair and reverse the damage. It's so common that, in accordance with Danish research, being alcohol-free for a day a week allows enough recuperation to lower the chance of developing cirrhosis. The NHS is more conservative and recommends taking the use of a few days to allow the healing process to take place. If you're contemplating whether your liver will heal in a matter of two or three days. But what happens if you are able to take a month off? The correct response, as per research suggests that drinking moderately can reduce the growth of liver fat by 15 to 20 percent. The stiffness in the liver is a sign of scarring in the liver may decrease in 12.5 percent.

The risk Of Infections FallsPulse is also increased once you start drinking. It takes only an entire month to see this boost - you'll probably notice a change in just five days. A study of people who drink at the end of the week in Ireland observed that following an overwhelming ending of the week, circulatory strain increased on a Monday but then decreased in the course of the day, before reaching an all-time low on Friday. Do not drink any more during the month, and it will remain in the low range or even decrease.

Being able to avoid it can also reduce the chance of developing Type 2 diabetes - a condition that is becoming a major issue in the majority of Westernized countries. The initial stage of the development in Type 2 diabetes is significant levels of glucose (a type of sugar) in blood. One of the primary reason for this is that our bodies cease to react in the way insulin does which generally reduces the levels of this. However after a month without drinking alcohol in researchers from the New Scientist group discovered their blood glucose levels dropped to 16 per cent. As a contrast, those taking part in Royal Free's Royal Free preliminary found their ability to respond to insulin increased by 28 percent.

Blood cholesterol is also lower over the course of a month which is a significant step in improving heart health.

As with the benefits for your liver there is a chance that you will not notice or feel any changes. However they're taking place as well as your body would be grateful to you for them.

Quitting and your weight

What if we change our course towards something you'll be able to do with the possibility of determining if it occurs - weight reduction.

Healthy people lose around 7lbs (3kg) when they go without drinking for the duration of a month. You'll probably figure out the reasons without motivating: alcohol is a source of calories. Seven calories per gram when you must be precise, cut down on drinking. It is possible to eliminate these calories and that in itself could cause you to slim down.

What percentage of calories will depend on the drinks you drink regularly? Most of the time the solitary portion of spirits mixed with eating ritual blenders is considered to be the moderately calorie-conscious drink, with around 60 calories per glass. the greatest calories are in mixed drinks which mix 4 to 5 shots of spirits in smooth or sweet blenders; they can be up to 200 calories in a glass. But, be careful in your drink choices if they don't the use of words or umbrellas at the top. Two huge glasses of wine can have about 370 calories, which is around five percent out of the 220 calories that a woman needs to consume every day.

However, as well as there are calories in alcohol are to be considered and consider, there are also the calories from the foods consumed as a result of alcohol. In recent times, it's been discovered that while drinking, our minds are at ease to detect food odors appealing - possibly to encourage the eater to eat. This can reduce the speed at which alcohol is absorbed by the system. In this way regardless of whether you're not expecting to indulge in a flurry of food before you start your evening out, the aroma of the nearby chip shop while waiting for your ride home can be extremely appealing even if alcohol is present in your system.

Alcohol also stimulates appetite through bringing down glucose and at the same time reducing the capacity to control your actions. If alcohol enters the brain, it shuts down our ability to make rational choices. It's like out the blue, a kebab you'd never consume calmly appears to be an extremely intelligent idea.

If you've recently consumed three or four glasses of wine or have a healthy body, the damage could end there. However in the event that you're susceptible to post-effects, you may be expecting a calorie explosion following the day.

Have you ever been through an acute hangover, where all you want to do is curl up in bed with a cup sugary tea, and wrap your body weight in bacon-stuffed sandwiches? or that no matter if you're able to eat as you awake and you're eating your way to England at noon. In reality, after effects don't only cause headaches the appendages shake and your mouth is like the inside of an animal's cage. They can also alter your eating habits. They affect you as they send your glucose falling. When we sleep our bodies get energy by storing sugar glucose stored in the liver. However, the proximity of alcohol impedes this happening. This can cause you to get up with an additional drop in glucose levels, which at this time triggers your body's start craving food fast to replenish your energy.

It's not like you'll all the time go for a bowl of mixed greens right now. sweet food, stodgy foods or even greasy food items are likely to be the food that causes the most stress when making a the decision. There's no reason to believe the reason for this. Some experts say that alcohol depletes levels of essential unsaturated fats that are found in our bodies and you can interpret this need for healthy fats as a need for any fat as well as a request to help from your body. fat digestion creates bile within the liver, and bile triggers your body to break down alcohol. In any case the case, it's equally probable that it's mental as the majority of us eat meals that are oily or seared with a sense of comfort, something you require to feel when you experience an effect.

Drink alcohol for a month however, you take away the calories you normally consume from it. You keep a safe distance from the fats you find from your churning because you're not feeling as alert or you feel like a little unclean the next day the effect is likely to be weight loss. I suggest it however, as the possibility of replacing drinking alcohol by sweet beverages, the, with calories , the effect will be restricted. If you truly want to lose weight by avoiding alcohol, it's a good idea to stick with soft drink waters and diet drinks whenever going out.

What is the amount of calories in your favorite beverage?

175ml glass of wine that contains 13 percent - 15 calories

A 125ml glass of sparkling wine with 12 percent - 90 calories

The 330ml jug contains 5 percent lager. 142 calories

A huge portion of 16 8 ounces of ale at 4 percent which is the equivalent of 91 calories

A huge amount of 16 ounces 4.5 percent juice, with 108 calories

One spirits (without blender) (without blender) - 61 calories

Margarita - 214 calories

Cosmopolitan - 116 calories

Martini - 204 calories

Pina Colada - 245 calories

Daiquiri - 203 calories

STOP QUITTING AND SKIN

Take a look in the mirror - or, far more importantly, take a selfie before you stop and take a look at your appearance for up to 14 days following the fact. You'll notice a change in your mood. It's possible to appear five to ten years younger.

The reason for this is that alcohol can be seen to alter the appearance of the face. Drinking alcohol causes blood vessels of your body get larger, and in the area of the face where the skin is thin there may be the cheeks becoming red the jawline and a small blushing around the eyes. If you see this happening regularly and you don't think that it's unusual, but when you stop drinking you'll see that your skin is less bronzed and your eyes appear more attractive.

It is also possible to notice that your face appear slimmer with each passing month. This is another symptom of the veins that are enlarged, which release watery liquids into the surrounding tissues, resulting in an increased puffy face, particularly at the beginning of the day. When you take a break from drinking, the liquid is drained away and your face begins to thin.

Alcohol also dries out the skin. A less hydrated skin is more likely to display fine wrinkles and lines. When these wrinkles stout up it will be a return to how you look. However, you might notice noticeable changes in the lines that run between your eyebrows. They may blur or disappear throughout your time off and, in some people , it could appear like they've had Botox!

To understand the reasons behind it, we must the study of Traditional Chinese Medicine. It is believed that the irregularities in the body are seen on certain parts on the face. For example, problems with the lungs can be seen on the cheeks, and the jaw is connected to the Ovaries. The forehead area is associated with the meridian of the liver. This means that if you overindulge in alcohol you may notice lines form here. If you're a regular drinker, they might remain there for a while. But if you stop, they will disappear. I'm able to reveal to the world that when I give up alcohol, I do one of the main aspects is that I am able to

The thing I noticed is that the area between my foreheads is more smooth. In Chinese treatments dark circles that appear under the eyes could indicate that your kidneys are bit over-worked. These also disappear during the month of your absence. It is possible to tell if you are drinking alcohol.

Chapter 11: Drink or Don't Drink

Imagine you're attending a birthday celebration with your best friends and one of the lovely service girls came over to you with three glasses of wine. Then, immediately, your friends were able to take their glasses with smiles and sipped a glass. They thank the server.

There is one glass left, and obviously it's for you and you must take it. The beautiful woman is staring at you in anticipation of your choice.

A glass of wine shouldn't be a danger, right surely, wouldn't it?

Here's where things get difficult. You shouldn't even touch the cup if you've consumed alcohol during the day.

However, I doubt that you'd refuse the glass, even if you've consumed as many as three bottles of beer earlier in the day. It's a fact that have all lacked the healthy tolerance in relation to alcohol.

It's because alcohol is widely accepted and is a popular issue in all cultures. It's the subject that frequently causes debate on the internet, mostly because it doesn't carry the same negative labeling that drugs as cocaine have. Certain people enjoy alcohol, and some don't, however most people are neutral. Everyone believes that drinking a small amount doesn't harm anyone.

On one side, it's been suggested that moderate amounts can improve our health. However, alcohol is thought to be extremely toxic, addictive and extremely harmful for our organs as well as productivity.

However, alcohol's negative effects are different for every person. It is influenced by many variables including genetics, quantity and kind that alcohol is consumed. However, let's leave that out for the moment.

STAY A MINUTE! What is ALCOHOL?

Despite the fact that alcohol is a well-known psychoactive substance, it has significant impacts on our mental state. Many people who drink aren't sure what alcohol is, or how it works. But, it is important to understand alcohol's effects on our bodies. It's essential that we study the chemical structure of alcohol.

The main ingredient in all alcohol drink available is the substance known as "Ethanol". It is the only type of alcohol that is readily available and is the one that can make you drunk when you drink excessive amounts.

It is produced commercially through the distillation and fermentation of sweet foods like grains and grapes. In its purest form it's clear at room temperature and has an aroma that is pleasant.

Ethanol has higher calories than protein and carbohydrates. That's one of the main reasons it is not possible to get pure alcohol in the majority of beverages that are available in the marketplace drinking alcohol in its pure form is dangerous because just a couple of grams can cause blood sugar levels to reach dangerous levels.

How the MAGIC The Drug Work!

After drinking alcohol, approximately 95% of volume is absorbed into the stomach and intestines directly into the bloodstream. Factors that determine the speed at which your body absorbs alcohol include:

Your sexual partner

How much food do you eat?

The level of caffeine in the drink you're drinking

If you're drinking wine, whisky or beers.

Since ethanol isn't dissolved in fats, males have greater muscle mass and less calories than women. It's clear that males absorb ethanol much faster than women.

Foods, particularly fatty ones and carbonated beverages that are noncarbonated reduce absorption. The more astringent wines absorb faster than beers.

The best part about alcohol is that, once it enters your bloodstream, it is able to move through and exert remarkable effects on all of the organs. It is, however, more favorable to the brain in comparison to the rest of your organs.

It's evident when you look at it.

If you're wondering why it's doing this. Our brains consist of two kinds of neurons. We have excitatory neurons on one hand and on the other hand there are neurons that are insular that are found in nature. Together they work to form the incredibly complex network of pathways that control all of our body's functions.

Ethanol is an natural depressant, acting on a large number of neurons.

Ethanol works primarily on inhibitory neurons that are found in our brains. It does this by reducing excitatory neurons' actions and also stimulating inhibitory neurons.

Many organizations, like the University of Chicago Medical Center: Alcohol and Anesthetic Actions believe that ethanol is able to increase the effects of neurotransmitter GABA which is the main inhibitory neurotransmitter that is found in the brain. The increased levels of GABA causes an increase in endorphins within brain cells, and can make us feel relaxed and euphoric.

However, it's not the only thing. Ethanol influences the brain in general through the targeting of specific centers within the brain, like the limbic system, the cerebral cortex and cerebellum among others.

Cerebral cortex, also known as the most advanced part of your brain. it takes in the information that comes directly from your sensory organs, and maintains your consciousness thinking processes and regulates the lower levels of your brain.

Alcohol reduces the inhibitory centers within the cerebral cortex, making you more impulsive, talkative and less socially repressed. It also reduces the speed of processing and thought processes, which raises your threshold for pain as well as affecting your ability to judge.

Alcohol can boost confidence and allow you to do things you shouldn't do.

The limbic system comprises centers that regulate your mood and memory. Ethanol is a stimulant to this center and makes you vulnerable to extreme emotions like depression, anger and even aggression. Additionally, you are susceptible to memory loss episodes.

The cerebellum is the brain that coordinates your movements and it's not immune to the effects of alcohol. Ethanol affects this specific portion of your brain, creating a disordered movement and causing laughter.

All of these effects are related to the dose. They are only more noticeable when the amount of alcohol present in the blood rises.

In the lower concentrations the ethanol is a pure substance that gives the wonderful feelings of joy, confidence and exuberance. But there is a fine line that is easily crossed when the concentration rises. This is evident when you drink too much alcohol at a rapid pace.

Everyone makes this mistake and the reason is that a small percentage of us are aware about the way our bodies handle alcohol.

HOW FAST CAN YOU GO?

All alcohol you consume is broken down by the liver before being excreted out through your kidneys. This requires complex biochemical enzyme systems like the p450 system, as well as plasma enzymes, such as alcohol dehydrogenase. I'm not going into the specifics. The only thing you should be aware of is the fact that they are extremely slow when compared to the way we consume alcohol.

According to research that a typical person's metabolism for alcohol will be in a rate of 15 milligrams per deciliter hour.

In simple terms, this means that it takes an hour to process the equivalent of 15 ounces. This amount of drinking alcohol as follows:

400mls of regular beer.

300mls malt liquor.

Wine 150ml in each bottle.

45mls shot of spirits distilled (gin, vodka, tequila and rum whisky, whiskey).

Now, you'll be able to clearly see the issue! What is thought to be a small amount of alcohol can be a lot for a single day. The body eliminates alcohol slowly, and there's no way to stop this.

If you drink more alcohol than you are able to eliminate it. It gets accumulated in your body and instead of bringing that happiness you've always wanted. You're confronted with feelings of depressing, and the feeling of stupor and confusion.

However, does this mean that you shouldn't drink alcohol?

I don't believe there is an answer that is easy on this issue. I think the answer lies to drink in moderation. Alcohol has been linked with certain positive effects on well-being.

I believe it's crucial to consider the advantages because it can help us in the discussion about addiction issues in the future. It's true that alcohol can be both good and harmful.

It's good in moderation but is extremely harmful when it is misused. Now, let's take a look at both sides of the coin and address the following questions.

Is ALCOHOL SAD FOR YOU?

Let's look at red wine.

Consuming moderate amounts of red wine has been proven to provide incredible health benefits. Red wine is a great source of powerful antioxidants, such as proanthocyanidins and resveratrol. Fun names, I know.

Red wine is produced from crushing the dark grapes, and then fermenting it. Grapes are high in resveratrol as well as other substances that help reduce the effects of oxidative stress on the body.

Resveratrol is a component of the grape's outer layer and has been associated with many health benefits including lowering the risk of cancer and heart disease as well as fighting inflammation and cell death.

The research further emphasizes that people who consume around 150ml of red wines per day have a 30% less risk of developing heart disease than people who drink no alcohol.

If you're wondering why it works it's because a small amount of red wine can help in retaining the healthy high-density lipoproteins present in blood, thus reducing the risk of developing heart disease. The result is lower bad fats and higher healthy fats. Damage from oxidative oxidation and the dangers of reactive species that damage tissues is also minimized due to the action of antioxidants.

Additionally, drinking 3 to 4 glasses of wine each week can help lower the risk of suffering from strokes in older people and could reduce blood pressure.

The consumption of red wine and ethanol in general, are associated with other health benefits like;

Risk of dementia reduction The consumption of 10-30 ounces of alcohol daily has been proven to decrease the risk of developing dementia and Alzheimer's disease.

A lower risk of cancer Moderate consumption is associated with a lower rate of ovary, colon and prostate cancers. Skin and prostate are also less likely to be affected.

A lower risk of depression an analysis of middle-aged people has revealed that those who drink under 8 glasses of alcohol a week are less at risk of developing depression.

Lower risk of developing type 2 diabetes that affects 8percent of the population around the globe It's a condition that is characterized by high blood sugar levels that are abnormally high. Research suggests that middle-aged women who consume 1-2 glasses of wine a day have a lower chance to develop diabetes.

Other: moderate amounts decrease the risk of blood clots or birth defects, overall anxiety and stress levels.

All of this being said it is clear that drinking alcohol can be beneficial for your well-being. However, this is only true if you drink moderately.

I'm not going to lie that this isn't easy. It's easy to consume too much alcohol. We are going to examine some of the negative effects of taking alcohol.

Are you at risk?

I don't need to explain that drinking too much alcohol can make you feel sluggish. It's obvious. If you consume greater than thirty grams ethanol per day, it's nearly certain that you'll die from your liver one day.

If you are able to remember, your liver processes every ounce of alcohol you consume. If you drink too many drinks, your liver gets stressed and ill. The disease begins with the condition known as fat liver, where the liver gets stuffed with fat.

If you persist with the insult the inflammation of the liver cells begins to set in, cells begin to die, and dead cells are replaced by fat cells.

If the condition is chronic when the cells in your liver continue to die then they are replaced with fibrous tissue, instead of fat. It's enough to say that once this happens, a condition known as "Liver Cirrhosis" will be ended for that particular liver. It's irreversible and can be life-threatening in a couple of years. It's actually one of the most significant reasons for death among Western countries.

There's more.

Your liver isn't the only thing which is at risk. Alcohol consumption is generally harmful. Although moderate amounts can be helpful to reduce depression, excessive drinkers are more likely to suffer from more depression.

The same is true for cardiovascular disease as well as diabetes. moderate amounts of alcohol can lower the risk of developing it, however it has proven that men who use alcohol to excess even as low as 2-4 drinks per week are more likely to be at risk of developing diabetes, and even sudden death.

There is also the issue of dependency. Consuming alcohol frequently can easily overindulge and result in alcoholism. I'm sure you wouldn't want to be in that situation. This book is about fighting this habit.

How much is too much?

A normal drink is what you need to drink if intend to ever drink alcohol.

A typical drink per each day, for females and 2 drinks for males is perfectly fine. The problem for many folks is that they don't have any idea what a normal drink is. And , it's quite easy.

In many countries, a "standard" drink is any drink that has 15 grams of alcohol.

If you drink only fifteen grams alcohol each day, not more than four times per week. There's a good chance you will gain more benefits by drinking alcohol over the long run.

But, I doubt it. Alcohol is highly addictive. The more you consume it the less pleasure you feel from the identical amount you previously took. Also, the greater amount of alcohol you'll need to consume to experience the same feeling of high.

After a short time the addiction will begin to develop since you'll be constantly required to consume increasing amounts. Plus.

This is the reason for the cycle that many people find themselves in is drinking.

It is likely that you are in the same spot at the moment.

You're trying to quit drinking so much however, you'll find the bottle in your hands.

I have written the book in order to assist you overcome this addiction. Being a former alcohol user I am well aware of this negative spiral. I was in that for years. Many years of going back and forth between the bottle.

The positive side is that there's a variety of strategies that can help you beat alcohol dependence and I'll share them all with you. It is important to be aware of how alcohol affects you in order to fight its dependence which is the main reason behind this section.

In the next chapters, you'll discover more about how addiction begins, the most common mistakes you can make and amazing strategies to get rid of it permanently.

It sounds good, right.

Chapter 12: Dealing with the effects of Alcohol Withdrawal

As was emphasized in the previous chapter, the process of overcoming alcohol dependence involves a complete cessation of the consumption or abuse of any ingestion substance that contains alcohol. However, it is likely to have unpleasant results. Refraining from alcohol once your body has developed a tolerance to alcohol will lead to a condition known as withdrawal syndrome.

The withdrawal syndrome is an outcome of abrupt loss of alcohol from the blood stream. It's characterized by a variety of physical signs. Be aware that this is the point at which your mind and body are craving alcohol most strongly -- surely a major obstacle in your path to full recovery.

The symptoms of withdrawal syndrome are:

1. An overall sensation of uncomfortableness. Patients aren't sure the way they're expected to be feeling. They do know that they are agitated and are plagued by an uncomfortable feeling.

2. Cold sweats.

3. Nausea.

4. Foul body odor. While your body is going by the detox process it is possible that you're emitting an odor that is particularly unpleasant.

5. Vomiting.

6. A rise in heart rate or palpitations.

7. Fever.

8. Irritability.

9. Volatile emotional state. A feeling of discomfort could result in a failure to keep emotional control.

10. Bowel movement problems.

11. Nightmares. In addition to hallucinations, you might also suffer from

terrible nightmares more often than normal.

12. Trouble sleeping.

There are different degrees of withdrawal symptoms dependent on your level of dependency on alcohol. A majority of cases are manageable. The most likely scenario is that you'll experience symptoms for one few days or for a month. After that, symptoms will disappear by themselves.

The withdrawal syndrome isn't something that is to be overlooked. It is an essential component of the treatment process -- the last step before you are able to get your life back.

Be aware that severe withdrawal syndrome cases require medical attention. There are medical clinics specifically for such cases. In such instances patients are treated with different types of medications to ease the body and ease the general discomfort. It is advised to consult your physician prior to starting detoxification. If the withdrawal symptoms you experience get unbearable or don't fade after a while, make sure to consult with your doctor and seek assistance.

Chapter 13: The Treatments for Alcohol Use Disorder

A disorder of alcohol use is what medical professionals refer to as when you are unable to control the amount you drink and you have difficulty controlling your mood and controlling your feelings even when you're not drinking. Many people believe the only way to deal with the disorder is to use determination as if it's an issue that's an issue they can overcome on their own.

However, alcohol dependence disorders is a brain illness that affects the brain and makes it difficult to quit. The idea of treating it at home may be difficult and unsuitable.

The first step is to find out more information regarding the treatment option you want to choose, and you'll find plenty of options to pick from.

Concentrate on your Doctor

The term "alcoholism" (not an official medical word) is a type of alcohol-related disorder. E.g that people abuse alcohol, but don't depend on it.

A medical professional may suggest you suffer from alcohol dependence when you:

You think everyone else should drink.

Can't control your drinking habit.

You look awful if you aren't drinking.

When you meet with your doctor, you should discuss your concerns and your goals. Do you require drinking less, or stop drinking completely? Together, you'll be able to create an appropriate treatment program. Your doctor may be able to refer you to specialists who can aid you.

Treatment Options

Most of the time, the most effective treatment for you will depend on your specific circumstances and your objectives. Many people prefer the combination of extremely efficient treatments. You could get one by scheduling an appointment with your physician who will discuss with you the best treatment option. Effective treatment usually requires that you be admitted to an inpatient or rehabilitation facility for a period of time. There are alternative treatment plans that allow you to be an outpatient by obtaining assistance from the nearest rehabilitation center near your home..

Consult a physician

If you suffer from an alcohol-related disorder that is severe this is the most crucial step. The aim is to quit drinking and allow your body enough time to flush the alcohol from your body. It may take a couple of days or even months.

A majority of patients visit the rehab or hospital to seek help for symptoms such as:

Shaking (tremors)

Being able to perceive or see things that aren't actual (hallucinations).

Seizures

Doctors and other experts can observe for you and prescribe medication for the signs that you're experiencing.

Talk to a Therapist or Counselor

When you suffer from alcohol dependence Controlling your drinking can help greatly. You should also try to acquire new techniques and methods of managing your life daily. Social workers, psychologists or alcohol abuse counselors can teach you how to:

Think about the drink you are drinking.

Cope through stress or other triggers.

Make sure you have support from a system.

Note down your goals and make them attainable.

Many people require an incredibly short and brief counseling program. Some may require one-on-one therapy for a long time to deal with issues such as depression or stress. Alcohol can have a significant impact on the people around you, which is why a the therapy of your family or partner could aid too.

Medicines

There is no medicine that can "treat" alcohol dependence but there are some that could aid in your recovery. They may make drinking less enjoyable which means you won't like having to drink as often.

Disulfiram (Antabuse) can cause you to feel sick after drinking.

Acamprosate (Campral) could aid in reducing urges.

Naltrexone (Revia) block the feeling of high you get when you drink.

The use of drugs for other ailments such as pain, smoking or epilepsy may also be connected to alcohol dependence disorders. Talk to your physician to find out which plans will best suit your needs.

Join a Group

A group therapy or support group can help you in your rehabilitation process and help you in following the instructions when you return to normal.

A group therapy session, with a therapist will provide you with the highest quality treatment with the assistance of others who are also users. Therapists aren't able to influence groups They are a group of individuals who have overcome their alcohol-related disorder, for example, Alcoholics Anonymous, wise recovery, and many other programs. Your group will be understanding and give advice, and assist you to meet your obligations. Many individuals remain in such groups for a long period of duration.

What to Expect

Recovery can take a long duration, which means you could require ongoing treatment. A few people in recovery have a relapse, and then drink again, but not all who is sober for a minimum of a year has a relapse.

If you fail, don't begin to believe you've failed. It's the first step to recovery and will make the process of recovery much easier. Five years later, just one in seven suffer from problems with alcohol. The treatment can be successful if you take your time.

Chapter 14: Medications for Alcoholism Treatment

It is important to recognize that there isn't a "perfect cure" that will magically remove your desire or desire to drink.But the positive side is that there's various medications that have been approved by the FDA that doctors can prescribe to combat alcoholism.These medicines can assist reduce the desire for alcohol and drastically reducing the amount of drinking days.They are most effective when they are paired with psychological and social intervention such as those offered by the AA 12 Step program.

But you also need to note that in spite of the current understanding that alcoholism is actually a persistent medical condition, there are still some people who believe that alcohol dependence and abuse are moral failures which can be conquered by sheer willpower.But medical experts in addiction firmly believe that medications should not be considered as substitutes for drinking alcohol.Rather, medications should be prescribed to aid in making the difference between a successful recovery and relapse of an alcoholic.They can work best and be most effective when taken with psychosocial modalities.Currently, there are 3 drugs for the treatment of alcoholism that are FDA-approved.But there is also a 4th drug which has shown potential in recent clinical trials.

Antabuse

More than 50 years, Antabuse has been approved by the FDA to treat alcoholism.As as such, it's considered to be the most effective medication on the market for this purpose.Antabuse works by limiting the body's ability to take in alcohol.In specific, it hinders the production of an enzyme that allows the body absorb acetaldehyde which is the product of alcohol breakdown.

If your body does not have the enzyme to break down acetaldehyde and acetaldehyde begins to accumulate in your system , even when you consume a tiny amount of alcohol.This is then accompanied by uncomfortable adverse effects like nausea, palpitations and flushing.You may imagine Antabuse as the reason you choose to avoid drinking alcohol to avoid the adverse effects.Antabuse isn't going to eliminate our desire to drink.You are still able to experience those "good effects" from alcohol but you'll eventually be at a point that you begin to feel sick.You may also think of Antabuse as as a "chaperone" for those who attend social gatherings at which there will be alcohol-based drinks.When you begin to feel the adverse effect of taking the medication you'll be aware that you need to stop and you won't have to be very sick.

Medical experts recommend prescribing Antabuse because they are aware that the consumption of the drug can be tracked whether at in your home with your spouse or another family members or in the alcoholism clinic.Some doctors are hesitant about prescribing Antabuse since it's not in accordance to what they consider the most effective way to avoid recrudescence, which is complete abstinence from alcohol.

Naltrexone

The medication helps to reduce the pleasure an alcohol-dependent person gets from drinking and the desire that causes the individual to go out and purchase more alcohol.Naltrexone can do it by blocking docking sites, or receptors for endorphins in the brain . Also, it works by blocking the protein production by the body to help in elevating mood.Those particular brain receptors are those that are able to accept other drugs such as heroin and morphine.Doctors generally recommend that Naltrexone take one pill a day.But the FDA recently approved the first time every month dosage of the injectable version.

In contrast to Antabuse, naltrexone is able to treat the root of alcoholism, or addiction.Alcoholism is the term used to describe a state in which you drink alcohol, you are enticed to consume ever more it.When you first start drinking two drinks, you'll find it difficult to stop after having at least 10 drinks as you are seeking the benefits associated with alcohol.What Naltrexone does is break this positive feedback loop, which allows you to have two drinks and not feel the need to have.

Certain clinical studies have proven that oral naltrexone may assist in reducing the amount of relapses into heavy drinking . Heavy drinking is described as having 5 or more drinks in a day for males and four or more drinks daily for women.In the study Combining Treatments and Behavior Interventions for Alcoholism COMBINE project, that was funded through NIAAA as well as the National Institute on Alcohol Abuse and Alcoholism It was discovered that naltrexone could be effective in treating alcoholism, up to twenty session of counselling for addiction with with a behavior expert.It is essential for that naltrexone be administered under the supervision of a medical professional.

Many doctors today prefer Vivitrol which is an injectable once-a-month form of naltrexone. This is because it lets patients stick to a medication they can only take every month.

Campral

Campral is a medicine that is taken orally 3 times every day.The medication is primarily a part of the brain's chemical communication systems.It is also recognized to alleviate the withdrawal symptoms associated with alcohol such as anxiety, restlessness, insomnia and unfavorable mood changes that could lead to relapse.Different scientific studies, as well as the clinical trials in Europe have demonstrated that regular consumption of Campral can boost the chances of a person being able to stay away from alcohol consumption for a period of weeks, or even months.

However, some research studies conducted within the United States and a COMBINE clinical trial indicate that there aren't any obvious advantages to using Campral when combined in combination with naltrexone, or taken alone.But it has been stated that patients who participated in clinical trials conducted of Europe were more heavily dependent of alcohol than participants in U.S. studies. studies.It was also reported that most of participants with the European clinical trials have not drank for longer amounts of time prior to starting Campral.The NIAAA said that these two factors could be responsible for the differences in findings.

Topamax

The FDA has granted approval to Topamax to treat seizures however it is not a suitable alcohol dependence treatment.Topamax offers the same functions similar to Campral and may also aid alcohol users in the same way, by reducing or eliminating effects of drinking abstinence.

The use of medications alone is not enough to cure alcoholism.

The above drugs are the most effective when used in conjunction with psychosocial treatment.They are not considered to be as effective when taken alone.There are three types of psychosocial therapy which experts have deemed to be extremely effective in alcoholism treatment.All of them have roughly the same rate of success.

Cognitive behavior therapy.It is a kind of psychotherapy that concentrates upon the use of a diagnostic tool to identify and the modification of patterns of thinking and negative thoughts.

Twelve step facilitation.A well-known illustration of this is Alcoholics Anonymous wherein patients are advised to follow 12 steps.

Motivational improvement therapy. This method is regarded as person-centered. A counselor will try to encourage you to consider and articulate your motivations to change and help you develop an individual plan to assist you make the necessary modifications.

Chapter 15: The Super Self-Confidence Spell

In the nineties, I was a part of a successful radio show that featured the comedian Geoff Carter. A hugely entertaining character who was able to walk in any space and everyone was watching his. The king of jesters and he is courtly unlike anything I've witnessed before or since. He exudes confidence and charisma and charisma to the point that when he was the warm up man for a major broadcasting station in Liverpool The on-air talent would complain that he made them look ugly. The audience would shout and applaud for Geoff to return to the stage. This was extremely disruptive to the fragile egos of high-paying presenters who were supposed be the hosts of the show. Geoff taught me how to present on stage and how to interact with with an audience. I'm not afraid to admit that prior to meeting Geoff, I was apathetically average when it came to performing and speaking in front of an audience live.

If you spend a whole day at the exact same place that Geoff is working at and in the evening, any conversation you hear will almost definitely be about Geoff. A few of the things I have witnessed him do as a form of entertainment such as being seen in a five star hotel completely naked, save for a costume that he put on to make a comedic Halloween. on. He has also repeatedly been able to offer all patrons in bars complimentary drinks by pretending to be a member of the production company for TV and convincing the proprietor who runs the place that he's searching for locations for an upcoming show (you become the hero when you offer people drinking free drinks it seems) and he has even was crowned winner of an award on a nationally telecast UK TV game show dressed as a 10-year-old school boy, wearing shorts and a Dennis the sling style shot.

Geoff and I have never decided to join forces and fate just happened to throw us together in the same moment. He was already employed by an radio station named Magic 999 and I was employed by the station's larger sister station, Rock FM.I had volunteered for a promotion to a higher level shift at my own station. I was thrilled, but slightly anxious, on a Friday afternoon, I was summoned into the office of the manager to hear the news. The Programme Controller for the two radio stations was an extremely tall 6'7" relaxed man named Mark Matthews. I grew as a child listening to his radio show in my home town of Darlington and was somewhat stunned by the thought that I was working for Mark Matthews. When I sat at the front of his office desk, I sat there, he shut my door (always an issue I've discovered however if the mail arrives late, I am worried).

Without a smile or chatter, he went straight to the point and informed me that he had positive news and some bad news.

I requested the negative information first, and he informed me that I wasn't promoted to the position I wanted. I was shocked as it meant that I would be in the late-night show that I was sure was not my style. I felt like I was being cheated as I had racked up some impressive listening numbers and felt I'd logged the right amount of the time on this anti-social shift.Before I had the chance to protest, he informed him that host of the Morning Show of Magic 999 had been fired and that I was to be promoted to that post. I was to be working alongside Geoff Carter and our new team would begin on the next Monday at 6 am!

Radio isn't like that often two strangers are chosen and then thrown into an studio, and instructed to entertain. In contrast to television, very minimal, if any research or testing is conducted. This is what makes it exciting however, it is very risky too. If security of job is important to your life, then I wouldn't suggest the career path of broadcasting. If you don't begin delivering an increase in audience within a year, then it's you who is the one who gets replaced. This can be a challenge since radio is a specific profession and, often, to be able to find your next job it could require you to travel hundreds of kilometers across country. This is not too hard if are a single person, but if you're a father like me, did, it was a huge pain. It was a matter of selling the house as well as taking your kids out of a place they loved, and telling your wife goodbye to her family (again). In the twenty years I worked as a commercial radio DJ, we relocated 16 times, and my kids attended several schools.

This Beck and Carter morning show was an ideal storm. My dry and somewhat darkly observational style humor merged with Geoff's outgoing larger-than- life persona to create something special on the air that barely is seen in our day. The sister Station Rock FM was a cash cow and was therefore the main issue for the management, which resulted in Geoff and

I were granted the freedom to do whatever we wanted to on the air. The atmosphere was chaotic and the result was a risky radio show. It was dangerous in the best way, but you never realized what would take place next, and we didn't! The crowd was massive because the majority of them did not want to shut off the show to avoid missing an amazing moment.

On a spring day during the program, the reporter who was a serious and very serious young man named Stephen Saul was finishing reading the half-hourly news bulletin from the third microphone at the back of the studio. The final piece that is usually lighter-hearted is about the impending solstice celebrations for the summer. The author told us about the druids were planning to gather at Stonehenge (a ancient monument located situated in Wilshire, England) to recreate a pagan ceremony that will ask the Gods to grant a summer of abundance. They would perform a dance in the open air and if they succeeded, the entire country will get a glorious summer over the following forty days.

When Stephen was finishing his bulletin as he straightened up the tie (he was the only one at the event to dress in this manner), Geoff announced to the audience of 70,000 that Stephen was going to perform the identical dancing naked on air prior to 8am. This was a ridiculous notion because no one was more likely to be a part of this kind of thing more than Stephen Saul. What the listeners could see the jingle of the radio station was played before the song began was Stephen insisting on his position and refusing to be a part of the humiliating stunt. After much debate and argument on air , Stephen finally agreed to dance in full dress. Geoff was never able to forgive his dance partner and said that he was responsible for the weather that was so terrible this summer.

What is the fate of a man like Geoff when you mix in alcohol? Let me tell youthat carnage is what happens!

Geoff Carter and I worked in a bubble of non-reality. Our lives were totally detached from the regular 9-5. The time we would leave work was 10am every day, and the majority of our colleagues had completed only the initial hour. ours was almost completed. We soon became acquaintances, partly due to the fact that the show required it and also because nobody could find anyone else to play out at 10 am on Tuesday mornings. Don't let that statement confuse you. We were not children of the moment... My age was late 20s and Geoff was a year older me.We were mature enough to understand the rules.

Alcohol became the central point of our relationship, it was the way we spent our time together. We would go to the pub before 11am the majority of times and we would stay until 6pm at the latest. After lunch, some of the 9-5ers from the office would walk into the pub and we would greet the crowd with a cheer. Then they would remain for their time as Geoff as well as I would keep them entertained. Some returned at 5pm, after work, and find us drunker but less interesting, lying on the bar, having been drinking throughout the day. We were generally drunks who were happy who never caused problems and mostly dropped things and shouted off into the crowd. If Garter arrived, it was a different story , and there was always trouble once Garter came in!

Garter was the somewhat odd name Geoff was known by when he was drinking badly. A character that was so distinct from the genuine charming Geoff that it might be a completely different person. Garter was a grumpy person who was just as unpredictable to spend time with, as it was to be to play with live grenades. A variety of unknown drinks caused the alter ego to emerge and, when it did, the day would often end in tears. Garter was insanity-drivenly protecting his friends and drink buddies. The situation could get nasty simply because he figured that somebody outside of our group was taking us seriously in a humorous manner. Geoff was a friendly but tough man and I remember thinking that if something ever happened, I would not have anyone else on my on my side in such a scenario. But, I'd have to counteract this admiration by the fact that he'd likely be the cause to the problem at the beginning.

In the end, after a long and thorough study and unwavering determination to the cause, we discovered that two beer brands have polarly opposite effects on him. If he were to drink Brand A all night long it would leave him being in the gutter, crying like an infant. If he consumed Brand B all night he will become aggressive and may cause us to be in trouble. The trick we devised was to switch the brands. It must always have Brand A followed strictly by Brand B. Drinking this way helped us maintain an level. However we never did us think about stopping drinking, it would have been unthinkable.

Our relationship could seem to you as incredible entertaining or shockingly bad manners depending on your own viewpoint. I can say that it was fun when I was younger and I'm sure our 9-5 colleagues were jealous of our unconventional life style. Every day was a new childish adventure that provided us with wonderful colourful and dramatic tales to tell the world about our adventures the next day.But there's a dark beneath the surface of my drinking life. It is clear that this wacky, funny guy is not my personality at all. I'm not an reckless fool who is constantly being kicked from bars. I'm not a comedian who sits on the bar's top and holds the court. It's not me, and for those who know Craig the real Craig it must be similar to watching someone fall into mental disease.

Imagine that someone you love transforms into a person with all the personality traits and character traits that you admire in a matter of minutes. They go from being the person you have known and trust to becoming a stranger with no recollection of their past. Consider if the man I've just described to you is the type of person you'd like as your husband or dad of your kid?

I was suppose to play both characters while drinking with Geoff. Craig is the real Craig is an honest, hardworking and creative person who has been a reliable father to his children. The drinkers in bars and pubs got free entertainment by watching the banana skin fall of a slapstick comedy-loving family members went through the loss of someone they loved and knew. Alcohol is in complete compliance with the laws of nature and adds the 'yin' to each 'ying'. However stunning the illusion may appear, keep in mind that it is just an illusion. it is! If people claim that they drink to boost their confidence or to make them more social, they're getting caught up in a different trick to get high.

Alcohol is in reality an anesthetic, disguised as something much more attractive. Each aspect of our character is perfectly adapted to serve an objective.

Infringing on this beautiful design and altering an element of your character using an ingredient is the worst thing you can do.

Yes, everybody feels uncomfortable when they enter the presence of strangers. However, understanding that this isn't an indication of weakness, but rather an natural response to our development from more dangerous times is essential to be at ease with it. Social anxieties and shyness are just the brain's way of exaggerating certain risks and generating characteristics to guard us that aren't useful in our modern times. It's only the time that makes this part of the mind appear to be an inability. When we were hunters-gatherers and were required to hunt for the food we ate, sources, we were in a more dangerous and dangerous environment. Today , we are coddled by our surroundings and it's extremely unlikely that while you wander through the mall , a wild beast will jump out and take aim at you. Yet, the social phobic feels the 'fight or flight feeling in this setting and feels uncomfortable and not helpful. Yet, a long time ago, this exact mental state could have been an essential character trait. The person we consider to be an individual suffering from social anxiety is the one most likely to be able to survive an attack.

Everyone suffers from social anxiety, but on different levels. In extreme situations, it can be a crippling illness that makes daily life challenging, but on a normal level it can have a significant impact. Many people do not can be confident enough to show on a nightclub with a clean slate and go to the dancefloor. Dance floors in nightclubs are ghost towns until sufficient alcohol is consumed by patrons. It's odd since alcohol does not claim to increase self-confidence because of the consumption of alcohol. When you consume alcohol, it alcohol has no connection with self-esteem. It simply affects the vital part of our brain's chemical system that is intended to ensure your safety. It lowers your inhibitions, and decreases your ability to assess and judge the danger. Many people say that they feel more confident after a drink, but they're more stupid! It's like feeling confident due to the surroundings that they are in, but what should I take this person out of the bar and put they in the middle area of an eight-lane motorway during rush hour and instructed that they had to avoid fast-moving vehicles and cross the road in safety, will they still be able to describe the feeling they felt as confidence? It's unlikely, since they'll most likely be crushed under an auto!

Another example of how absurd it is to say that alcohol boosts confidence in people Consider this scenario: you're admitted to a hospital for an operation and the surgeon is summoned on the wards to check on you prior to taking you to the operating theatre. While he talks to you about the procedure, you can see that his hands are shaking with anxiety and fear. Conscient of his insecurity and not wanting to make you be scared, he calmly reassures you saying , 'Oh, don't worry. I'll have an enjoyable drink before we begin"!

Are you content to continue with the procedure?

Alcohol can create the illusion of confidence , as it limits the field of vision. It only gives you an extremely narrow view of what's really taking place, and hides the truth from you. Racehorses may have blinkers that stop them from becoming distracted by things happening within their peripheral vision. They are able to concentrate on what's directly in their view. Alcohol employs the same method to block your attention from the slight of hands going to your rear. Alcohol actually causes a type permanent brain injury we mistakenly call confidence. If it was really an enhancement in self-esteem,, you wouldn't be witnessing the horrifying consequences that result from the wrong assumption of what's going on within the brain. A lot of unplanned pregnancies would not have happened, and a correspondingly large number of careers wouldn't have been destroyed by a "confidence-driven" mistake at the office Christmas celebration.

There isn't any confidence with this trick the way the rabbit wasn't in the hat at all. As a self-help equivalent from Penn and Teller, I want to defy the rules and explain how this illusion of alcohol is accomplished.

Chapter 16: Finding New Habits

When you finally put down the bottle and you've decided to put the sauce aside for good, you're going to have to develop some new and more effective ways to keep you entertained while keeping your mind stimulated. It is crucial to keep your mind active as long as you can to ensure you don't become bored. In fact, boredom can cause relapses and you do not want this to occur. You'd like to be engaged, so that you're not even having the time to drink.

A key part of staying engaged is keeping your brain engaged. If you can keep your mind busy and occupied with other activities this can help stay away from drinking. This step is as crucial as keeping your mind busy. An unfocused mind may start thinking about old thoughts and then to think about getting the bottle. If you keep your mind busy and distracted by other topics this will assist greatly in your efforts to remain sober.

Hobbies and interests

Okay, now that you realize that you must stay active and keep your mind engaged by establishing new ways of living The following step is to identify what interests you have and then find a few hobbies that you can keep yourself busy. Everyone has interests , and you can turn those interest into a hobby. It is important that you pick new hobbies you're enthusiastic about and enjoy so that you stay inspired to continue to pursue them and not become bored or uninterested.

So , what are the types of activities that you really like doing? Perhaps you'd enjoy any of the sports you enjoy or, if you're interested in crafting and arts, you might want to enroll in some craft classes. If you're short of funds there is usually numerous inexpensive or free activities that are available in your location that you can take part in.

Volunteering can be a beneficial idea. There always are charities, organizations and non-profit organizations who require volunteers You'll discover that helping others who are in need could be rewarding for you, too. It's generally easy to locate places that require volunteers. Churches and activity centers could be a great starting point.

When the weather is pleasant it is common to find spots outdoors that will keep you busy and entertained. You can take a stroll or bike ride, an jog/run in your favorite park, or play tennis or basketball on the courts you like best. If you're the kind that enjoys getting fit, you can combine your love of exercise and healthy eating and make it into an activity. Join a gym, and start an exercise routine, and make it a part of your daily (or at least once a week) life. If you can't pay for a gym membership, there are many options you can exercise at home as mentioned in the first section of this book. It is possible to turn your exercise into your own hobby if you're passionate about fitness, which is definitely something to be proud of.

Whatever your passions and hobbies are, there are activities that will fill your time, and also replace your time that you'd otherwise spend drinking.

In the end, while the AA meetings are an excellent way for people to quit drinking but there are a few guaranteed ways to quit drinking alcohol completely without having to attend the AA meetings. With the help of family and friends and online support groups, as well as by eating a healthy diet, getting active and pursuing different and exciting hobbies it is possible to quit drinking and stay clean for a long time.

Chapter 17: Helping and Help and

Assistance and support are important. It doesn't matter if you choose to seeking it through a therapist outpatient programs, rehabilitation and self-treatment or even hospitals. All you have to do is not to take it on by yourself. Finding people you can count on for advice and comfort, or even encouragement is a huge accomplishment. Take into consideration that you had a problem with alcohol and are now trying to adjust to the change in your life.

The assistance or support you need is possible by relying on counselors, friends, family members along with co-workers, as well as other health professionals. These steps can help you in coping with the help and support to take care of yourself:

The first step is to establish an effort to build trust with friends and family. This is a resource which is essential for getting back to health. If you've fallen short of your loved ones before , you could take advantage of family counseling or couples therapy. All you require is an arm to support.

The development of a community of friends that are clean provides you with another advantage. Connecting with new people can do this even if you've been around a drinking lifestyle. Being with friends who are clean will ensure that you've been able to support your journey to recovery. You might consider joining a group of civil society or church group, and attending social events and taking part in social events.

Consider shifting to a house with an alcohol-free living. This will guarantee that you are in a place that is secure, welcoming, and comfortable for you to live in during your recovery process. Be aware that you are dependent on alcohol, and therefore you'll require a safe and comfortable environment to ease the stress associated with this. This is where you can find an alcohol-free space to live in.

The final step is to ensure that you attend regular meetings. This should be the top priority. This could be a time that meets to talk about the negative effects of alcohol and its aspects so that you can constantly be informed. This can also help ensure that those you spend the most time with are aware of what you're going through as you work towards recovering and healing.

Chapter 18: Simple Tips To Quit Drinking

Congratulations on deciding to stop drinking. Making a change to a habit, particularly one that is addictive isn't effortless. It requires a lot of willpower, effort and motivation. It isn't a quick process. If you've made the decision that sobriety is for you, it's time to end your drinking. In this article we will explore some easy and practical ways you can follow to end your drinking.

Quit Cold Turkey

The most risky way to stop drinking is to go cold to the point of quitting. Quitting alcohol suddenly is like taking off the imaginary Band-Aid. The cold turkey method is perfect for those who drink socially or casually. But, if you're physically dependent on alcohol, you shouldn't stop cold turkey until your doctor has recommended it.

Write it down

What are the reasons you'd like to quit drinking? This is a question that needs a lot of self-analysis. It is not possible to use the same reasons used by others to stop drinking. In the case of recovery and sobriety, it is personal and personal. Every experience is different between people. So, it's the right time to make the list of reasons you'd like to quit drinking. Maybe you're looking to live more healthy lifestyle or enhance your relationships, or simply want to be more relaxed. Whatever your motivation take note of the reason. Even if it sounds like a bit silly for you, do not condemn yourself for the reason. Every motive is important. Each of these factors can give you the drive you need to stop drinking. It's not solely about changing your lifestyle and a change in your mindset towards yourself.

Keep a Diary

Another method of keeping yourself on track is by keeping a journal. The decision to stop drinking is a significant change in your lifestyle. It takes your body and mind a bit of time to adjust to living a life with no limits on alcohol. If alcohol was an integral element in your daily life, then the period of time to accept and acknowledge all this may be more. Keep in mind that this is for your personal wellbeing. Begin keeping a journal to record the emotions and feelings you experience. If in the past you drank to relax after a stressful day, you can keep a diary to serve as a way to relieve your anxiety. When you are tempted to drink, take an entry in your journal.

When you're done, begin taking note of all the events that led to you desire to drink. Take note of the different things such as people, events, or feelings which prompted you to think of wanting to drink. Add as much detail as you can regarding everything. If you take note of all this, it will be more clear the way that your body and your mind react to alcohol. This will allow you to recognize your triggers for alcoholism that caused it initially. The process of addressing the triggers becomes simpler when you know what to address.

Set an Objective for Drinking

If you've decided to stop drinking, or would like to completely stop drinking Then you should set your own drinking goals. A drinking objective in this context does not mean that you're allowed to drink alcohol again. Instead, it refers to how long you are able to be without drinking. If you're given alcohol, it can help control your emotions and feelings so that you do not allow yourself to drink.

If you're looking to limit consumption, in the ideal you should establish a limit on how much alcohol you consume. You could be a fish in a barrel but it's not ideal for your overall health. In the end, you're trying to get back the control over your life, don't you think? So, set a limit. When you have establish a limit, make sure that you adhere to it. Be careful not to set this limit excessively high. There's no reason to be setting a limit such as "I will quit after having six drinks." This defeats the goal of setting a goal in the first place. Review the guidelines in this book regarding the ideal drinking limits , and make an effort to adhere to the guidelines. Reduce the time between your drinking sessions. After some time, it is easier to cut down on your consumption of alcohol without becoming restricting. If you're not sure about your drinking limit be sure to talk with your physician regarding the issue.

Drink slowly

If your aim is to decrease your intake of alcohol or you're looking to limit your drinking habits, you should begin taking your drink in small doses. It is not necessary to gobble down each drink presented to you. Drink your drinks at a slow pace as you can. If you're looking at stopping drinking, don't consume any alcohol even a little. Instead, choose a soda, fruit juice or any other non-alcoholic beverage. Whatever you drink take care to drink it slowly and do not be in a need to consume it in a hurry. It can cause you to feel that you're having more drinks than you are. Additionally, it's ideal for keeping the company of your drinking friends and to not be left out. If you do drink alcohol, make sure you make sure you don't drink with a full stomach. Be sure to drink plenty of fluids while you drink.

Don't Keep Alcohol at Home

If the temptations are always around you and you are constantly surrounded by temptations, the likelihood of drinking a lot and often will rise. What can you do to quit drinking if you're constantly surrounded by your preferred bottles every day? It is now time to get your home cleaned and get rid of any traces of alcohol. Consider the process as spring clean. Eliminate all alcohol, and do not keep anything in your home. Even if you're determined to quit, the urge to drink can hit anyone at any moment. What are the reasons to consider taking the risk? In some cases, boredom could be a reason to drink. To prevent these kinds of situations later on, you should not drink alcohol at home. This also aids in limiting the amount of alcohol you drink.

Change Your Attitude

It is vital to begin changing your outlook on your life, yourself and alcohol. If you've used alcohol to control your emotions or to manage stress or due to an related health issue, you should begin to address the problems. After you address the root of the issue it is easy to quit drinking. It is also the best way to begin to reduce your dependency on alcohol regardless of whether it's emotional, mental or physical. Your life can be everything you'd like it be and you do not need alcohol to accomplish this. For instance, if you were a person who used to drink alcohol due to the fact that it gave you confidence and confident, change your mindset towards yourself. Improve your self-confidence and stop drinking alcohol to protect yourself.

Days without alcohol Days

If you're attempting to stop drinking alcohol, start with small goals you can set for yourself. Begin by setting a goal to not drink for at least a week. When the week is done and you've completed the week, inform yourself that you're not going to drink for two consecutive weeks. Do this until you're able to go for as long as you could without a drink. If you're reducing your consumption of alcohol, create a schedule of alcohol-free days you. If you're planning to consume four drinks in one week, then make sure that you don't consume alcohol daily and don't drink at least three times every week. It allows your body to adjust to a lifestyle that doesn't involve alcohol. When you have achieved your goals, you'll feel more at ease with your life. It will provide you with the desire to stop drinking completely. Be aware it's only you person who can accomplish this on your own. There is no one else who is able to take over your life. You have the power to control your life, no matter your beliefs at times.

Beware of Peer Pressure

Peer pressure is a real thing and can be found throughout your life, no matter the age. Peer pressure isn't just limited to teens. Even in adulthood there is a chance that you will experience this type of pressure. Don't succumb to peer pressure, no matter the stress you experience due to it. Be aware that people who try to force you to drink may not have the best intentions in your heart. Friends may try to persuade you to drink another one since they enjoy having a drink with them. If they are truly your acquaintances, they will be able to accept that you're not going to drink. The most effective way to avoid being influenced by your friends is to learn to not say no. This isn't only about learning how to say no, but you should establish boundaries for yourself. These boundaries make sure that you take proper care of yourself.

Request Assistance

Reducing your drinking and avoiding drinking is the commitment of a person. There will be occasions that you'll would like to satisfy your desire to drink. This is why you need an established support system that will stop you from doing this. Your support system can give you the motivation and the willpower to continue to push through in times of feeling particularly down. Inform your loved ones that you are in desperate need of their help. Start speaking with your doctor, counselor for alcohol or therapist regarding your need for assistance.

Keep busy

Get involved in all those activities that you haven't done because of your alcohol addiction. Now is the time to get back to all your activities. If you had certain activities you put off due to the fact that you were not able to make enough time because of the recovery and drinking and so on, now is the time to get going. Get your schedule as full as you are able to. Enjoy time spent with family and friends or work harder or anything else that doesn't allow you the opportunity to begin thinking about drinking. If you're absorbed in your work, the likelihood of you drinking or even contemplating drinking will be drastically reduced. It is also the best way to boost your overall efficiency. After a while, increasing your productivity can also boost confidence in yourself and your self-esteem.

Stop the temptation

If you know of certain areas and people which make you want to go for a drink, you should start by avoiding them all. If you're familiar with relating drinking alcohol to specific occasions like holidays or vacations, holidays, devise the best strategy to handle everything ahead of time. Make sure you are aware of your feelings and manage those emotions and anxieties instead of resorting to alcohol to deal with them.

Don't Give Up!

Whatever you decide to do, the only thing you can't abandon your goals. If you're trying to stop drinking, then keep working towards the aim. Even if you do slip up every now and then, make sure that you work towards your goal the next day. Don't create the habit of making these mistakes. If you're facing challenges, setbacks and repeated relapses in the path to recovery Do not give up on yourself.

You don't need to start taking all of the steps in one go. Start by incorporating these guidelines into your daily routine gradually. Start by taking step by step and don't try to tackle everything in one go. One sure way to slow down your progress is trying to tackle everything at once and then rushing into it. Do not rush Take your time and don't be stressed. Once you've started using these steps, you'll notice a positive change not just your attitude but in your life overall.

Conclusion

When you are able to overcome your addiction, your treatment will focus on creating a better meaning for your life, and assisting you to keep your alcohol-free lifestyle in the future. When the treatment is performing its job, it's your responsibility to follow these things:

It's almost a given that you'll be prone to feelings of euphoria and hunger along your way towards recovery. To fight these, it's beneficial to get enough sleep, eat well and exercise regularly. Additionally, these activities can help you reduce stress and improve general well-being.

www.ingramcontent.com/pod-product-compliance
Lightning Source LLC
Chambersburg PA
CBHW070100120526
44589CB00033B/1009